A GUIDE
to
BEING
a
BETTER *BEING*

Dear Jagshree Rao,

Wishing you deep
peace, faith and joy
on your journey
to the Light,

With love,

Maggie

A GUIDE TO BEING A BETTER *BEING*

A GUIDE

to

BEING

a

BETTER *BEING*

Maggie Richards

For The Beloved

You were always there, before the start,
Then gifted me a beating heart.
Through infant cries you held me tight,
Blew on me Your holy light
And gave the kiss of destiny
To lead a life most heavenly.
Of work and words, strength and silence
Joy and goodness, gifts and guidance
So that others, too, may come to know
The beauty that we're here to show:
That love, our Home, is always there
Inside, boundless, for all to share.

CONTENTS

PREFACE

To better understand life – and therefore ourselves and one another – requires an insight into reincarnation.

In reincarnation (literally, to be made flesh again) we're given the opportunity to learn the rules of Earthly life by experiencing all facets of it – being male and female, rich and poor, abuser and victim, and so on – until we achieve balance.

Any rules we break and lessons we fail to learn in a lifetime are given to us again in another life, with the cycle continuing until we assimilate the lessons and progress on our evolutionary path; a road of self-betterment. Equally, the skills and knowledge we develop in previous lifetimes may be stored in the bank of "me" as wisdom, passions, gifts and latent abilities.

Originally a journalist, writing for the likes of *The Times* and *The Guardian,* in my 30s I discovered a gift, if you will, for deep meditation. In that liberating state I found myself presented with glorious glimpses into other realms of existence. Every time I "went" to one I was changed.

Later, I was taught how to journey at will into the non-physical realms, where I'd be blessed with clarity, hope and guidance from beings of the highest order who'd long won the game of Earthly life. The pure love they emanate continues to transform me, and others too.

Today, as a London-based Somatic Experiencing trauma therapist, meditation teacher and writer, I help people from all walks of life nobly be the best they can be.

INTRODUCTION

We are guests on a quest
To bless and be blessed

My earliest memory isn't actually a memory. It's a knowing; a timeless, wordless knowing that I'm not from here. I'm *just visiting*. A tourist on Earth, if you will.

So where *am* I from? And why am I here? So keen was I to learn about life that I arrived six weeks early, on 14 February 1976. This was in west Wales, to a kind-hearted 40-year-old antiques dealer mother and a witty social worker dad who'd been told by doctors they wouldn't have any more children.

Saint Valentine – did you know? – was a 3rd-century Roman bishop and martyr. He was imprisoned, beaten and eventually beheaded on 14 February for refusing to renounce his faith. Now that's a mighty love!

I began practicing my deep thinker look early on.

2

As innately happy as I was, life dealt its inevitable corrective blows. Between the ages of six and 18 I was sexually abused and assaulted – including an attempted rape – by several males. The first abuse, coupled with my parent's lack of emotional attunement to me at the time, eventually closed me down. An iron cage of rage, unworthiness and emotional pain enclosed my heart.

In time I became manipulative, mean-mouthed and sometimes downright cruel. My body suffered, too. For years I held my bladder, endured lower backache, and ground my teeth at night.

Yet through it all I instinctively knew there were happier times to come: all I needed to do was to keep forging ahead on my search for healing. My faith got me through, even after I almost died aged 18, when, thousands of miles away from home, in Canada, I was taken to, but mercifully escaped from, a gang of rapists.

Seeking comfort in the warmth of the sun's rays days later, an image of a candle flame appeared clearly in my mind. Intuitively I understood that I was being offered a profound choice: snuff out my light and pass over now, or live and continue on my life path. My mind turned to my family and I decided to live.

Enough strength was given for me to return home and gain an English degree, followed by a diploma in journalism. This led to a move to London to become a professional journalist.

Shortly after a new start in the capital I accepted a press invitation to a life-transformation workshop that lived up to its billing. Remarkably, what I was to experience on that course had been revealed to me in 'psychic flashes' when I was a girl.

Experiencing it finally 'in the flesh' triggered an uplifting decade spent experimenting with all manner of healing modalities and spiritual processes, including, at 30, a life-transformation week that opened my heart and helped me let go of a great deal of past darkness. Better still, I discovered the ennobling balm of meditation, and with it, an inner call to help others.

This intense phase of self-betterment led, when I was 34, to the arrival of my Spiritual Teacher. Now true spiritual training began, marked by ennobling tests of asceticism, obedience, celibacy and emotional and psychological trials so severe that at times I felt I was on a torture rack.

The rewards? So many! Not least, clarity about where I'm from and why I'm here. Many of the awe-inspiring answers apply to us all, for life is a team game that will be won when equilibrium has been achieved for *all* beings.

Today, I am a kinder, gentler, wiser and more knowledgeable being to a degree that I never imagined possible. I've not only forgiven those who abused me, I've even become grateful to them. Without experiencing their iniquities I wouldn't have been compelled to rise above my darkness, and in doing so discover my purpose.

It was karmic to be abused, and from such I learned valuable lessons.

It was my free will to let myself be fooled by the rapist's charm.

It was my destiny to realise I was never a victim.

This happiest of perspectives I achieved as a neophyte; a beginner on The Spiritual Path. This very honest guide to potentially becoming the best possible you reveals my spiritual unfoldment so far. I hope you enjoy it and benefit from it.

I wish you well,

Maggie
<u>maggierichards.co.uk</u>

CHAPTER 1
MEDITATION

Listen to Me in silence
And I shall give thee guidance

Imagine for a moment that you're seated in a steadily ascending aeroplane. All you can see through your window is dense cloud, yet you stay calm and patient, confident of your powerful upward trajectory. Suddenly you emerge from the clouds, and wow! – a paradise-like panorama of bright blue sky and glorious sunshine fills your vision. Clarity reigns. You are lifted!

Meditation is the aeroplane, the vehicle that allows us to transcend life's trials and gain a peaceful 360^0 perspective. Staying focused on the destination – the goal of self-betterment – is essential if we are to go higher and break through fear into the light.

Stilling the mind is both a discipline and a road to liberation, leading us silently and surely to the very best version of ourselves. Worry, anger, judgement, jealousy, selfishness and co. all prevent us from hearing the small, still voice within: the voice of the Divine. Quiet your mind and you begin to silence your inner demons, and tune into the Divine.

That inner guide – which surely all of us know at one point as an intuition, a persistent thought, a gut reaction or an inspired idea – takes you gently by the hand and leads you, if you're willing, to a compelling new realm called Transformation. There, joy soothes the sorrowful, strength fortifies the weak, laughter lifts the angered, and peace uplifts the grieving.

I desperately needed transformation in my 20s. If you'd known me then – a cheerful, London-based lifestyle journalist writing for the likes of *The Times* and *The Guardian* – you wouldn't have guessed that I was secretly tortured by feelings of abandonment, rage and despair. I knew I was loved but I still couldn't *feel* it. Manipulative and vulnerable, but pretending not be, I found it difficult to let anyone close. Yet I intuitively knew that whatever life was about, this inner hell was *not* it.

One day, sat at my desk at home, I thumped my temperamental printer after it refused to print for the umpteenth time. As my fist landed a blow on its black plastic shell, so did a realisation: it wasn't the machine that needed fixing. It was me.

I'd already had life coaching and NHS counselling, and in 2000 had done a life-transformation process called The Journey. That weekend in a Kensington hotel, I'd been chosen from among the 400+ participants by founder Brandon Bays to demonstrate her healing process live on stage. Sitting in front of a microphone, with blue-eyed Brandon stood beside me, I began answering her questions about the sexual abuse I'd suffered at the hands of a local teenager when I was just six years old.

For years as a child, just before sleep, while being aware that I was still in my bed in rural Pembrokeshire I'd 'drop' without warning into another scene: me on a stage, sitting on a bar stool, talking into a mic. Now, as tears poured down my face, an electrifying force surged through my being – *this was it!* *I'd been here before!* The Journey proved a powerful trigger; from now on I would use all my power to break open the iron cage enclosing my heart.

Over the years I'd gradually shut down my natural joy, as childhood sexual abuse was followed by multiple sexual assaults by various males, culminating at 18 in my being groomed by a rapist, who took me to a small, empty room in a tower block where five gang rapists were waiting for me.

Mercifully, he decided I was his sole 'property' and we went back to his flat. With help, I succeeded in escaping his tortuous attempts to rape me. But I couldn't escape his flat, and was held prisoner there for close to 24 hours. I eventually 'bought' my freedom by offering him permission to sexually assault me.

While The Journey helped me feel significantly freer and lighter, I clearly had more work to do to be truly happy. Much more. I now gave free rein to my curiosity, diving into Emotional Freedom Technique, Brahma Kumari gatherings, crystal stones, reiki healing, Neuro Linguistic Programming, a past-life reading, a life between lives regression, hypnotherapy, Metatronic healing, AIM energy balancing (still with me?), shiatsu, cranio-sacral therapy, Theta healing, a 'channelled' reading, tarot reading, foot reading, palm reading, Time Line therapy, The Reconnection sessions…

I tried almost every so-called "new agey" modality going. And I loved it. Each experience felt like peeling off a layer of darkness and made me feel better. More whole. More *me*.

Then, at the dawn of my thirties, everything changed again. I fell in love! I fell in love with meditation, and how I felt when I became still and silenced my mind. Meditation helped me discover a blissful peace inside, when – despite my traumas, failed relationships and family issues I had no problems. Not a single one.

Intuitively I knew that all the healing work I'd been doing had been preparation for this joyful juncture. All the time I'd been looking 'out there', and now – at last – like a secret, sacred reward for my tenacity, I knew that the way Home to the ineffable *something* I was seeking was inwards.

Meditation graciously found me at a spiritual centre in Cologne, standing with eyes closed, shaking my body to lyric-less staccato music among 20 or so adults, in a low-lit room in the Osho UTA Institute. Osho was a joyful 20th-century Indian mystic who created a new style of meditation specifically for Westerners who lack the bright-eyed spiritual heritage of Easterners. I'd done vipassana, or mindfulness meditation, before, but it hadn't given me this fervent thirst for more. Osho's meditations set me aflame inside!

With the dedication of a nun, I began meditating almost every day. Discovering my own ways of disengaging from my fear-based lower mind allowed me to shush! the yapping dog that would run indiscriminately after any flotsam and jetsam it noticed floating along the river of my awareness.

The results were life changing. I found myself worrying less about what others thought; began to express my true feelings more often; felt more at ease in my body; laughed and danced more; and became gentler with myself and others – men in particular. The knots of my past began to loosen, resulting in more energy, more connection with others, and more patience. Not a forte of mine, historically.

Where, in my early 20s I might turn to alcohol or recreational drugs to intoxicate myself 'out of' difficult feelings – only to have them return another day in a debilitating game of invisible tag – now I was finding a new strength to face the lows.

Resting in the sacred inner silence of meditation, the wheat in me would spontaneously separate from the chaff: self-compassion from shame, kindness from cruelty, resilience from rage. And therein lies one of life's paradoxes: *the stiller we become inside, the more our outer life moves in a positive flow.*

Inner peace, I came to realise, would not be achieved in the future, once I was married, owned a house, etc. It is achieved in the here and now, moment-to-moment, when I am loving, grateful and calm *despite* life's imperfections. Inner peace, then, is a perspective. A choice we can make at any time.

In November 2007 I signed up for an 18-month part-time personal development course in a small spiritual retreat called Osho Risk in rural Denmark. The trainees would meditate three times a day, every day. I couldn't get enough of the feeling that came at the end of the hour of deep relaxation; an enriching emptiness that signalled the release of my cares. I discovered that as the mind settles, the heart opens. Where judgment stops, peace begins.

So inspired was I by the effects of meditation that the following year I began offering meditation classes at home. Increasingly devoted to my spiritual life, I found myself going deeper into the inner realms, to the point where, during one most memorable day, my awareness expanded during deep meditation into what I can best describe as infinity, and a profoundly peaceful oneness with everything engulfed me. Held in that higher state, I wasn't thinking, or even watching my thinking. I felt like consciousness itself: at once everything and nothing.

It wasn't until 2010, when I began a strict spiritual training under my Spiritual Teacher, Cher, that I would be graced with transcendence again. Through Cher and her team I came to more fully understand that inner peace is ever-present. It is always there, reached through the gateway of the heart.

To get to and through the gate at will, we are called to master the restless lower mind or lower self that blocks the path to self-betterment by generating thoughts based in fear. We do that by purifying ourselves through meditation and other timeworn spiritual practices, such as ethical living and positive thinking.

As I focused on leading a devotional life, my clairaudient, claircognisant, and clairvoyant skills began to sharpen. I'd always been a 'feeler', sensing what someone was really feeling even if what they were saying pointed to the opposite. Since childhood I'd also been aware of an invisible guide that would communicate thoughts to me, sometimes as little premonitions, other times as intuitions.

Now, those latent abilities were raised up and strengthened to the point where I would daily experience the uplifting interconnectedness of the physical and non-physical realms of existence. It's true that we are not alone.

In prayer and meditation, I began receiving a great deal of loving assistance from guides and helpers in spirit, who I believe we all have. With time, even more powerful beings would come to offer guidance, among them Buddha and Jesus (who I've come to call Yeshua), despite being non-denominational in my beliefs.

This guidance tended to be communicated in the form of inner visions or inner journeys, sometimes as insights or instructions heard with the inner ear. At other times it would be prompts to take positive action, such as recommend a spiritual book to someone in need, or send flowers. Every message shared one ultimate goal: to help me polish up and be a better being. The better we are, the more we can help others.

I also learned how to psychically "tune into" a situation and shift it in a positive direction without physically speaking; how to use the power of numbers for a higher purpose; and heal with my thoughts.

Fallible me did get things wrong, though. Early on in my training, and still a bit green, I fell into the lower-self trap of questioning a message I'd received in meditation. To which Cher replied, 'As the mind rests in silence, the Divine can speak and be heard. Listen to the messages without questioning or trying to change their meaning to suit your level of awareness.'

Mindfulness versus meditation
Neutrally observing your present moment experience as it unfolds is the key technique in both mindfulness and deep meditation.

Mindfulness is an excellent foundation for deep meditation. In developing a good relationship with the higher mind (or seat of awareness), it acts as a springboard to our higher self. It is in living from our higher self that our relationship with the Divine deepens.

Deep meditation is a set practice enjoyed with eyes closed and your focus directed inwards – ideally to a point where your awareness is no longer tethered to your senses. Deep meditation is necessary to deepen our relationship with the Divine, which is the fullest expression of your potential – your very best self!

The more we live in tune with our higher self, the less harm we cause, and the less bad karma we accumulate. Karma is the law of cause and effect, action and reaction.

Balance and bliss are rewarded when there's no more karmic debt to pay. We build up debt – bad karma – each time we do harm to any being. And so, in our life's quest for betterment, we choose to include certain experiences and people in order to pay our debts and stop further negative action. However, because we don't normally remember the beatific bigger picture, we may perceive the challenges we face as unjust.

It is part of everyone's life quest to balance their karma, with the ultimate goal of unification with the Divine – the very source of all that is good, joyful, loving, peaceful and wise in us. The more karmic debt we pay off, the closer we become to the Divine.

I have always experienced and longed for closeness of one kind or another, and all my adult life had been yearning for someone to "complete" me. I fantasised of a Prince Charming who'd "save" me with marriage, a family and a big house in the country (dreams fuelled by my voracious reading of dad's eclectic library, especially classics by George Eliot, Charlotte Bronte, and Jane Austen).

Starting in my 20s, I was swept off my size threes by several Prince Charmings. A generous millionaire with a beautiful country house. An entrepreneur with private staff at home, who treated me to dinner at a Michelin-starred restaurant. A gentleman interested in starting a family, with whom I pootled around Paris.

While I fleetingly became enamoured of my suitors, meditation granted me the key to loving *me*. And as I developed self-love, the volume on the old nagging question "When will I meet someone?" gradually turned down – and would eventually switch off and leave me in peace. I started respecting myself, and life became much more relaxed and full of promise.

And so, here's something you may wish to ponder deeply: what if the love of your life was Life itself? What if 'the One' was not another human being, but *all* beings and beyond? What if what you long for most is right where you are, within you?

If you want someone kind, successful and faithful in your life, start being those things for yourself. Become the person you'd love to spend your life with and you'll never be disappointed in love again. In fact, you might just become very happy!

Psychic attack

A psychic attack is a paranormal event usually triggered by negative flows of energy in the unseen realms, sometimes deliberately invoked using rituals or magic, and sometimes arising from negative thought patterns – albeit unknown to the person thinking them.

Take a former meditation client of mine. In a group class one day his thought waves had built up so much negativity that they manifested in a set of arrows that lodged in my solar plexus chakra. He wasn't aware of what his lower self had done, and neither was I at the time. It was only when I felt out of sorts and later meditated on the root of my discombobulation that I psychically saw what had happened. I'd suffered an attack, despite using a protection technique (see Meditation Guidance, point 4) and leading an ethical life.

Because deep meditation involves entering other realms and interacting with other beings and entities, it's considered wise to protect yourself. Not all beings are of the light. Some may wish to take your light away, especially if you're making an effort to better yourself.

Just as in the physical world you can suffer anything from a slap to grievous bodily harm, there are gradations of psychic attack. My Spiritual Teacher was once dragged from her sleep and swung around in the air by a malevolent entity! If you suffer unpleasant feelings or find yourself assailed by sudden, strong negative thoughts towards yourself or someone else, and intuit it may be a psychic attack, you can help transmute the harm by praying to the Divine for healing, or seeking the assistance of a reputable healer.

If, when meditating, you start inwardly seeing, sensing or hearing things – colours, lights, energy patterns, images or even discarnate beings – it's a sign that your inner faculties are opening up. As best you can remain neutral and unafraid. And, if prompted, seek the guidance of a spiritual adviser. They can assist in understanding the hidden meaning of what you were shown.

MEDITATION GUIDANCE

1. Find your style

Some people reach inner peace through song or chanting, others through silently repeating a mantra, or being in nature. Still others learn to silence their mind by gently focusing their gaze on a candle flame. Seek out the type of meditation that works for you. When you've found it, you'll know.

2. Create a sacred space

Creating a peaceful space within your home dedicated to meditation can help significantly in cultivating a relationship with your higher self. Enjoy beautifying it with uplifting objects such as candles, flowers, or a photo of a beloved Spiritual Teacher.

3. Stay focused

Harness the power of intention to help you focus, so that your mind may rest in the Eternal Now. Gently focusing your attention on your heart space will help, allowing waves of love to gently well up from within. Have faith that those waves will soothe turbulent thoughts.

4. Protect yourself

Protect yourself from potential psychic harm by visualising yourself surrounded by a gentle white light. Ask the Divine to keep you safe. You may wish to imagine yourself surrounded by beneficent beings too.

5. Be disciplined

Ideally, make meditation part of your daily life, just like brushing your teeth. Mastering your mind requires commitment because your lower self has no interest in helping you be happy. It *thrives* off controlling you, causing you to accumulate bad karma. The more you meditate, the more inner strength you'll build up to help you stay calm and on course through life's highs and lows.

6. Tune into nature

The forces of nature are very powerful: visualising your favourite nature scenes can help to quiet your mind. See yourself meditating before a tranquil ocean, gazing at the setting sun, or resting in the serene silence of a forest, for example.

7. Make the most of mantras

Focusing on and remembering the Divine is imperative because it's the very source of your inner peace and goodness. Use the name that represents your Creator. Repeat the words 'I love the Divine / God/ Allah / Krishna or Buddha in your mind. A divine name used with faith and authority can both banish fears and doubts and expel an unwelcome entity from your presence.

CASE STUDIES
Work stress resolution

Abby, a great friend working in a highly pressured environment, struggled to tolerate the colleague who sat next to her because she found their behaviour disruptive. Working against tight deadlines, on projects that required high levels of accuracy, she found the constant drama from her colleague distracting and frustrating.

After years of different failed attempts at making peace with the situation, Abby was prompted to do a healing meditation of forgiveness. Focusing inwardly on an image of her colleague in a loving pink light, she felt a profound shift – she was now free of any negative attachment to the situation. Within days the strain left the relationship, and within weeks the colleague was moved to another department.

If there is tension between you and someone else, acknowledge that both of you are creating it, and realise that you have the power to change the situation. It's like pulling on a rope back and forth in a tug of war. It simply takes one of you to drop the rope and walk away peacefully for the dynamic to shift for good. Forgiveness meditations are a powerful way to change your perspective and find the peace needed to move forward.

Pet blessing

Pets are powerful companions and teachers, and sadly sometimes a person's only experience of unconditional love. So the life-changing decision to become responsible for a pet demanded divine guidance.

Sat upright in bed one morning before work, eyes closed, I stilled my mind completely, set the 'filter' of my consciousness to the subject of my future cat, and waited. Sure enough, I was shown a screenshot of gumtree.com and intuited I was to look there in 10 days.

On the 10th day I searched the site and was thrilled to see an ad for some very fluffy, very white kittens. It had been posted just a few hours before, and one of the little beings is now my sweet and loyal Lili.

Past life healing

Discombobulated one day, but with no obvious reason to be, I decided to meditate on the root of my emotions. I found myself in an underground cave and in a past life. I was a man. And in deep despair. I'd been left there to die, alone.

Then – what was this? A neat snout appeared right in my face! A small pig had come to care for me. It sat its weight in my lap so that I could really hug it, triggering healing tears. It was a real comfort and I was grateful.

Next I observed a handsome, healthy man step out of the body of the prisoner me. He went up some stairs, reached a door, and opened it to see a young child running towards him and jumping joyfully into his arms. Behind the boy was my wife. We were together again! Safe. A new start! I kissed them eagerly, and then my wife and I knelt in prayer, our little one bowed down between us.

CHAPTER 2
SPIRITUAL RETREATS

Renounce the world!
Witness love unfurled

Throughout the whole of human history, man has been called to retreat from the world and focus fully on spiritual practice in order to better himself and make a truly positive contribution to the world.

On witnessing suffering, death and disease for the first time, pampered Nepalese Prince Siddhartha renounced his family and worldly treasures, and fasted alone in a forest for six years. The following year he vowed to stay in his meditation spot beneath a bodhi tree until he'd transcended the karmic cycle of birth and rebirth and found enlightenment. He succeeded, and became Buddha.

Prophet Muhammad regularly meditated in a mountain cave for 15 years before Archangel Gabriel spoke to him; the sacred wisdom imparted laid the foundation for the *Quran*.

It was Christmas and I was 30 when I found myself on my first spiritual retreat: a 10-day silent Buddhist meditation in rural England. I'd split from my boyfriend the year before; an emotionally eviscerating experience that had left me literally wailing for days. Healing was in order.

So, while my family were unwrapping gifts by the fireside, I found myself trying hard to keep my thoughts in order amongst strangers in the strip-lit canteen of a country house in

Wiltshire. We'd all agreed to refrain from killing (meaning a delicious vegetarian diet), stealing, sexual misconduct (no sex or masturbation), lying, intoxicants, and drugs for the duration.

Every day started at 4.30am with an hour of mindfulness in a dedicated hall, followed by a minimum of another six hours of meditation before retiring to bed at 8.30pm.

Roger, one of our teachers, likened disciplining the mind to tethering a calf to a stake: at first the animal fights for its freedom, but in time it accepts its fate and lies still. My mind turned out to be a Pamplona bull. I found it impossible to focus on one part of my body for more than a few seconds before my mind charged off to more exciting pastures. But by the fourth day, sat in the winter sun, my mind showed signs of slowing down – becoming more country lane than motorway. I even began to feel cheerful.

Come New Year's Eve, my thoughts turned to friends, all dressed up and drinking Champagne, while here was I in a tracksuit, sipping fennel tea and looking forward to another early night. Yet no fear of missing out assailed me. Instead, I felt newly at ease with myself: my tenacity had been rewarded with contentment. (The retreat also gifted me a life-long friendship with my diminutive roommate, Sachi.)

The following summer, hanging out in a spiritual centre in Cologne in between freelance writing projects, a friend Natalia began talking about some personal development training held at a similar at a retreat in Denmark. Before she'd even completed her sentence I knew with certainty that I'd be doing the course. It was exactly if something had decided *for* me.

Fast-forward to November and I was stepping out onto the gravel courtyard of a small, red-roofed meditation centre, set in the rolling hills of eastern Jutland. Here, a brave new world of kindness, compassion and calm opened up to me. The centre was called Osho Risk, and I'd indeed come to risk much during my years of soul-searching there – not least my pride, judgement, spitefulness and selfishness.

The therapist training into which I was enrolled was divided into 11 weeks over 18 months – all taught in English. Like the other participants, I wasn't there to become a therapist so much as to better myself and, I secretly hoped, find my husband. On first meeting my group, I was disappointed that I wasn't attracted to anyone. So my nervy preoccupation raised its head high again on being told there was one more to join the training. Would they be the One?!

Faster and faster beat my heart as the pale wooden door to the group room opened and in walked… a raven-haired woman. My heart sank. (It turned out she *was* a soulmate, however, with karma to balance with me.)

I'll never forget those first weeks spent sitting on Back Jack meditation chairs in groups of three or four, listening to individuals I barely knew talking honestly about their feelings and openly crying. It was amazing to me that these other beings – even the burly Scandinavian men – were just like me: near-bursting with repressed emotions, fears, passions, vulnerability, and longing to break free of fear's chains. It was as if I'd been holding my breath for 30+ years and finally – *finally!* – I could BREATHE!

Two constants underpinned and embraced all the therapy: daily meditation and the unconditional love of the small band of largely Danish residents and locals who were ceaselessly welcoming, affectionate, honest and accepting of everything about complex old me, including my growing love of silence. Unlike anywhere I'd ever been, everyone and anything (except physical violence) was welcome at Osho Risk.

For six months, nine months, a year, I was met with unreserved kindness, until even my most stubborn fears and hurts surrendered in tearful gratitude to the sweet, steady force of the light there. I may not have found my husband, but I had found love again – with the people, the place, my own growing maturity. And the Divine. My diary entry for 8 May 2008 reads:

I would give up everyone and everything in an instant if it meant being with The Beloved. Zero hesitation! I would choose God.

Many skins were shed in that furnace of love, and what was revealed, glowing, at my core was a devotion to meditation, joyful happiness, feminine beauty, a love of dancing, and a passion for nurturing others and helping them find their inner peace. I completed the course in the summer of 2009 pretty much completely changed.

But still more healing was destined. At a reunion of my training group at Osho Risk six months later, Marianna, my dark-haired soulmate, gazed at me through deep brown eyes across the dining room table and said, 'It would be good for you to live here.' Silence. Then: a single tear.

Back in London, and for the next few weeks her words echoed louder and louder through my being. Though my life looked successful, I was lonely and unhappy. This new opportunity felt like I was running *to* something. Something truer than where I was, hence my heart saying yes! JUMP!

In March 2010 I ended the rental contract on my Victorian flat and sailed into a promising new chapter. I didn't know how long I'd be away or what would happen: I just knew I was leaving. I had total faith that I'd be guided to where I needed to go. First stop: Osho Risk.

My official status at the retreat was now as a worker. The excellent worker programme lets you stay there inexpensively for up to three months in return for helping with the running of the place for a minimum of three hours a day. Typically, this means helping prepare lunch or dinner for everyone, and cleaning one of the communal spaces.

I was to experience some of my most euphoric moments so far in the commune's little kitchen, chopping, slicing, mixing, stirring, frying, cutting, pouring – all to uplifting music, peals of laughter, and – on the best days – dancing! There was something steadfastly soothing about cooking together, for each other, with joy. It taught me that, done with an open heart, any activity can be a pleasure.

It was only now, with my work, social and romantic life peacefully contained within two small, simple buildings under a cinematic sky, that I understood how much effort my old life had been demanding of me.

London life had been hard on my spirit – spending time with friends and even just enjoying a hug would necessitate booking a diary date weeks in advance. Living alone meant I was responsible for all the bills, while working from home meant my days ran into each other, and I'd often snack on sugary treats to give me energy.

Life at Osho Risk, however, was structured: meditation at 7.30am, 5pm and 7pm, lunch at 1pm, and supper at 6pm. All my meals were healthy and homemade. Other residents took care of the maintenance of the buildings. And, apart from my mobile phone tariff, I only had to pay the modest rent, which I managed by freelancing as a writer. There was a wine cupboard upstairs for Saturday nights, and a big sunny room to dance around whenever the mood struck.

I came to realise that, paradoxically, it was the very strictness of this routine that allowed me to surrender and just *be*. Structure and discipline provided the boundaries within which I could rest at what felt like a quite magical level. The thought, 'I fancy a tea, but don't want to get up from the table,' for example, might float across my spacious mind, and moments later a friend would offer to make me one. Ditto having a hug. Everything became an effortless flow. And for the first time as an adult, I *felt* carried by Life. For now, all I needed do in order to receive such blessings was relax and be receptive.

Twentieth-century literary giant Franz Kafka puts it beautifully: 'You do not need to leave your room. Remain sitting at your table and listen. Do not even listen, simply wait, be quiet, still and solitary. The world will freely offer itself to you to be unmasked. It has no choice; it will roll in ecstasy at your feet.'

I ended up living at Osho Risk for nine months; the length of a human pregnancy – and the birth of a new me. Ta da! In an email to my friend Hazel I revealed: *I am loving my peaceful, joyful sojourn here. This is such a precious time; I am sensing more and more how rare a position I am in. To be totally without pressure to be, do or say anything, or go anywhere.*

I have broken away completely from old structures and am attaching myself solely to those that uplift my spirit. I am utterly my own mistress, with all the time in the world to surrender to the sweet, fruitful flow of life. Few people get this chance, and I am cherishing it... My life is ripe with possibilities and happiness.'

RECOMMENDED RETREATS

Osho Risk, Denmark, where I lived, and have co-hosted mind-body-spirit festivals, offers a full calendar of various trainings and workshops.
oshorisk.com

International Meditation Centre, Wiltshire, UK, where I enjoyed my first (silent Buddhist) retreat, offers free 10-day residential courses (though there is a suggested charge of £250) throughout the year.
internationalmeditationcentre.com

Findhorn Foundation, Scotland, UK. Although I haven't yet been here, I've witnessed the changes it has made in friends of mine, and I'm also fascinated by the way it was co-created with elemental forces.
findhorn.org

Chapter 3

Somatic Experiencing®
Trauma Therapy

The body houses hidden doors
Revealed to the mind that gently explores

Hurt ego demands to know:
Why did you do this to me?

Heart asks:
*What lesson am I meant to learn from this?**
*@jennagalbut on Instagram.

There are times in life when there's just too much going on for you to be able to hear the wisdom of your soft-spoken heart. Sometimes, our experiences are just too much: too fast, too soon, too awful.

Terror, anger and shame, for example, all create 'noise' in our system, preventing us from tuning into our inner wisdom. This manifests in all manner of ways:

- Psychologically, as negative repetitive thoughts – 'There's something wrong with me', 'I can't do this'
- Physically, as energy blocks – chronic numbness, pain or stiffness, for example
- Spiritually, as a lack of self-confidence, enthusiasm, and joy, for example.

By my mid-20s, the cacophony from all the abuse and bullying

I'd suffered had generated a near-impossible psycho-biological bind: though I yearned for love and intimacy, I'd keep men at arm's length with cruel words and mixed messages, terrified that letting a man close might 'destroy' me.

While I used my attractiveness to get attention and affection, I lacked the capacity to be consistently kind and loving. I was confused and in knots. Physically, much of me felt awkward and 'wrong', especially my thighs and pelvic area. I found myself out of my depth physically and emotionally, but without the tools to say no, so I'd over-ride my needs and wound myself further. Ouch.

As human animals, we share the same instinctual survival responses as prey animals, but our more complex brains and lives mean that fight/flight can easily be compromised.

Imagine a car crash in which the person gets caught behind the wheel; even before impact their body would be surging with survival energy, yet they'd have no way to defend themselves or escape.

When fight or flight and the triumph of saving our own life are thwarted, the brain's final intelligent survival tactic is to make us freeze; play dead. By shutting down our faculties, we protect ourselves from being overwhelmed by impossible feelings and sensations. And it works: we survive and get through it.

Being removed from the effects of life's pendulum swings towards pain and suffering comes with a price, however. When our capacity to feel difficult emotions is inhibited, so is our capacity to feel their polarities – uplifting and empowering states such as love, compassion and trust.

The freeze response can – if prolonged – lead to dissociation, where we no longer sense our reactions to our environment or our relationships, or we do so at great remove. Dissociation may result in blanks in our memory, or make it increasingly difficult to connect harmoniously with others: it means we no longer feel fully alive, and makes us prone to depression and/or fatigue.

Dissociation had been my way of surviving the numerous traumas I'd been unable to escape as both a child and as an adult. And, despite the cocktail of therapies, workshops and retreats I'd experimented with in my 20s, I continued to suffer many ill effects.

Thankfully, when I was 30, Somatic Experiencing (SE) came along, which stands out as the one therapeutic approach that changed me the most. With remarkable efficiency, SE quietened the anguished cries of my traumas, and from the new silence flowed profound healing.

As the anger I'd been turning against myself was released, compassion, self-respect and a growing ability to say no – to both my own negative behaviours and that of others – took its place. I was growing up and I was so grateful.

SE is a pioneering whole-person approach to resolving physical and emotional trauma, PTSD, anxiety, and stress-related conditions. Its primary focus is on what's happening in your body, because it holds keys to recovery that the (lower) mind doesn't.

Neuroscience now makes it clear that the body and brain react in specific involuntary ways to a perceived or actual threat to one's life. These discoveries help us understand that not only can we not (alone) talk our way out of trauma, but that talking about it too freely can actually lead to re-traumatisation.

So how does SE work? Based on observations of prey animals, which are routinely threatened with death, but never traumatised, SE helps to safely 'unlock' the primal fear-based fight/flight response in which a person gets stuck when experiencing an overwhelming event. It does this by guiding them back to the here and now through the embodied realisation that they've survived: it's over, and it *feels* over.

SE is the life's work of Peter Levine PhD, stemming from his multidisciplinary study of stress physiology, psychology, ethology, biology, neuroscience, indigenous healing practices, and medical biophysics. Peter argues that trauma and spiritual awakening are two sides of the same coin, with awakening coming on the back of traumatic experiences.

I embarked on the three-year professional SE training in 2007. It involves experiential group work and regular demonstrations led by the teacher. One day during my training, our tutor asked for a show of hands from those who had extreme sound-related symptoms, such as chronic tinnitus or misophonia. Up went my arm.

'I can't *stand* the sound of people eating noisily,' I admitted a little anxiously. 'Even my super-cute nieces when they were little: we'd be at the dinner table and even though they looked angelic, inside I wanted to kill them!' My eyes widened and my hands formed claw shapes as I confessed: I'd never understood why noisy eating had provoked such an extreme reaction.

'What's your favourite sound?' asked Larry, after I'd joined him at the front of the room, the 40+-strong group in a semi-circle to my right. 'Baby ducks!' I replied, smiling. 'What is it about baby duck sounds that you like?' he asked, smiling back.

Rapport established, he asked me about the sound I didn't like (others' eating), so that we could work with the high activation (fight/flight) behind my body's protective instinct, and work to safely discharge it. I don't recall* how we got from ducklings to my experiences in Canada, but I do remember his first response to my attempted rape story: 'That's a lot of people.'

Those few words directly unlocked my secret inner state. Yes! Six rapists – that was a lot of people! A *big* threat to my life. This was such a simple observation, but it was one that nobody had made before.

Having that very small but very significant part of my overwhelm acknowledged opened up a healing stream of relief. My shoulders dropped and I exhaled deeply as I felt for the very first time that I wasn't alone in facing those six men in a tower block. There was safety now. Support.

Of its own accord, my torso leaned forward and collapsed onto cushions I'd been handed. It felt a life-saving balm to body and soul, this surrender. Until that moment, my spinal muscles and viscera had been frozen in a likely constant state of terror for over a decade.

In time, Larry deftly led me to the realisation that sound of mastication was "overcoupled" – intertwined with – a repressed animal instinct to eat the rapists alive! To protect me, my biological self had wanted to tear them apart!

In that tiny room so far away from those I loved, I'd faced an impossible trap: being raped by a gang, or being subject to the sexual violence of my "friend" alone. So powerful was the warrior instinct to protect my life and my dignity that my nervous system protected me from even being conscious of it. Even when Larry again asked, 'Do you know what your mouth wants to do? They do,' (nodding at the group), I said no. I genuinely didn't.

But, in the privacy of my dreams that night, the truth was revealed in vivid scenes of a black panther, bright red blood dripping from its jaws. It had so much vitality! I realised with gladness that my murderous rage was not just a "no", it was also a "yes"! I wanted to tear at life, eat it, feel it, run with it! From that day, I began to stop grinding my teeth and holding my bladder at night. I was really healing.

As my understanding of, and compassion for, my blocks grew, so did my compassion for my parents in having to deal with their daughter being bullied and abused, and especially for my father's helplessness in being unable to protect me. Dealing with my anger freed me to be more loving and receptive to the love I needed.

Like ancient wisdom teachings, SE focuses on empowering the individual to transform fixation to flow, helpless to helpful, dark to light. It teaches us how to use our higher mind – associated with the pre-frontal and medial cortex areas of the brain that govern awareness, logic, and reason – to harmonise body, mind and spirit. In SE we learn to:

a) *detach* by stilling the mind and neutrally observing and reporting our own experience as it unfolds – without judgement

b) *attune* to the innate, non-verbal wisdom of our physiology – the same divine forces that, for example, heal a bruise and make hair grow
c) *face our fears* with support, clarity, and compassion. And move *through* them to a greater sense of inner strength and wholeness.

Meditation, mindfulness, The Spiritual Path and SE all use awareness as the primary navigation tool. All train the mind not to run away from the present experience, however painful or unpleasant, but to stop and simply *observe* it. This mysterious ability to be the witness of our own experience – in it, but not of it – responds excellently to being cultivated.

In 2012, his 70th year, Peter Levine PhD acknowledged in an email to Somatic Experiencing practitioners how, having started in his original 1972 class of about 15 people meeting bi-weekly in his Berkley, California 'tree house', SE had now been taught to more than 8,000 souls worldwide, and was destined to spread far beyond his personal involvement and continue to expand and change lives.

He went on to describe a dream he'd had 20 years ago, when SE had just begun to extend its reach. In it, he was approached by a Tibetan monk holding a treasure chest. Without speaking, the monk handed the chest to Peter, who took it to the adjacent room, which had a safe embedded in the rear wall. It was then revealed that it was Peter's role to place the box in the safe, which he respectfully did.

Peter had channelled a thread of ancient wisdom. The dream symbolised that his task was to keep this shamanic knowledge safe by translating it into a relatively logical system that was relevant applicable to our modern, scientific and trauma-filled life. When I described SE to a fellow aspirant, she responded: 'It's preparing people for The Spiritual Path!'

CASE STUDIES
Flight terror
Tony was determined to get his life back. Ever since an incident on a business trip, he'd become terrified of flying and had now become very fearful of even being outside.

In fewer than 10 SE sessions, Tony learned tools to help him change the signals his body was sending to his brain about being under threat. Using them daily, he quickly developed his capacity to be with his own fear, and with his own longings – to be safe, and to belong to people of warm heart.

Tony learned that when he used his whole body to hold the fear or other emotion, it didn't cramp his chest, or buzz around anxiously in his mind. He also learned to care for himself, noticing when he was becoming afraid or sad, stopping what he was doing, and for a few moments helping himself realise that in the present he was safe, and that any rush of emotion belonged largely in the past.

Soon he felt happier and more alive. He even began helping colleagues to notice when they were stressed, and offering them tools for calming themselves.

Chronic insomnia
Note: Ben had done other therapeutic work prior to embarking on Somatic Experiencing sessions.

For 26 years, Ben had suffered insomnia, and for the last four years a recurring shoulder pain that woke him up to three times a night. Through SE he soon learned to trust his body as a safe and relaxing 'place' to be.

Around the time of his fifth session, Ben started a new job, and within a week realised he'd made the wrong decision, which left him feeling very stressed. The job wasn't for him. 'I don't want to do it. That's enough.' Asked whether there was a time in his life when also he felt 'That's enough,' memories of his childhood began playing in his mind's eye.

The youngest of four, it was Ben's daily chore to lay the breakfast table for the family. It felt like far too much responsibility, yet he never felt able to speak up for himself. All the years of resentment and verbal impotence, we discovered, had been stored in his right shoulder as hidden defence movements.

Yet in slowly exploring, over a few sessions, the defence movement his arms had instinctively made (marking his personal energetic boundary with his outstretched arms, and making a calm, confident verbal declaration, 'That's enough! I'm not doing this any more') the burning pain in his shoulder began to dissipate.

In a new space of presence, he finally felt compassion for himself. Compassion flowed into deep, restorative sighs as accumulated layers of exhaustion from not sleeping deeply for half his life now surfaced. Today, Ben sleeps well and enjoys more peace, groundedness and natural energy.

CHAPTER 4
SPIRITUAL LIVING

The Divine wishes us to know that we have a long way to go,
But every day, in every way, the Divine's workers love us so
With their help, we're called to choose the light
To fight the holy fight with faith and inner might

Spiritual living is a spiritual science with a noble goal: transmuting one's karma and bringing more light to this world. The acme of spirituality and self-betterment is harmlessness.

The more harmless we are, the more in harmony we become with the eternal forces of love, which nurture only. For true love – that is to say unconditional love – is rooted in compassion for *all* beings, not just humans. It demands effort, tenacity and a good sense of humour. If you're not sure whether the Divine has a sense of humour, just look at an alpaca's face!

Before joining The Spiritual Path, I considered the foundations of a spiritual life to be meditating, having psychic abilities, loving a Master and being honest and happy. I've since realised that to be spiritual is to brush the comb of consciousness through every aspect of my life and being – because everything is connected. One. 'As above, so below, as within, so without, as the universe, so the soul,' revealed Egyptian Spiritual Master Hermes Trismegistus, who co-authored a series of sacred texts.

In meditation one morning I was thrilled to see a neon green, red-eyed tree frog in the Amazon rainforest appear in my inner vision, like the one on the cover of David Attenborough's 1979 book *Life on Earth*, which had inflamed my imagination as a girl. The tree frog communicated to me that when I was angry, it felt my anger. All that distance away. Wow!

Feeling remorse, I was beginning to see the fuller picture of the power we yield as human beings, and feeling remorse for the way we abuse it. I was being called to be more responsible for the energy I was emitting to the world day by day: in other words, understanding that I had a responsibility to be peaceful.

Seekers on The Path are, at one point, expected to be peaceful *regardless* of their emotions. Emotions come and go (from and to where is an interesting question), while peace is a force. An omnipresent, transcendent, limitless force that is always there, beyond the senses-based veil of the physical dimension. The more peaceful we are, the more we're protected from harmful influences that may drag us off our path.

Lead a good life, with joy, gratitude and faith and you'll build up real power – power no-one can take away from you. The simple techniques and practices revealed below – by no means an exhaustive list – are methods of purification; practical ways of "cleaning up" in readiness to be deserving of meeting your Creator – either in life through mystical attunement, or when you leave your body when you die. The purpose of a better life is to be ready at any time!

EIGHT KEYS TO A BETTER YOU

1. Be kind

'Universal wisdom flows through you,' I was once told in meditation. 'Use it wisely. Be kind to all beings, including yourself.' Kindness is a strength. (It requires no effort to give in to temptation or negativity.) Whatever it takes, please be kind. To yourself and others, including animals.

2. Be happy

This was Buddha's core teaching: he said if you wish to be happy, decide to be! If you don't like a situation, know that you can change it, or change your attitude to it. You have the power to do either invested in you by the Divine, along with a responsibility to choose wisely. Follow your heart and be and feel positive. Positive energy has power, like air and electricity.

3. Exercise gently

The body needs movement to keep it in good working order, just like machines need regular maintenance to keep them functioning at their best. Swimming, walks in nature, and yoga are all excellent pastimes for empowering your body, calming your mind, and even lifting your spirit.

If you suffer anger issues – you have too much anger, or conversely, you have weak boundaries and feel unable to defend yourself when you need to – consider taking up a martial art to channel your energy in a non-violent way.

4. Laugh and en*joy* life

Laughter is God's music it's said. So why not *use* it as a spiritual tool to lift you? Lay on the LOLs daily. Watch and listen to funny things. Regular meditation, too, helps immensely in sluicing away negativity to expose your natural joy.

5. Love everyone, harm none, trust few

This is divine advice. The esoteric perspective on trust is: it has to be earned. Trust your goodness and see it in others. But be discerning, too. Temper trust with wisdom. Let others show they are deserving of your trust before you open your heart, home, life or body to them.

6. Keep a peaceful home

Your home is ideally your sanctuary, in which you naturally relax and bond with loved ones. Enjoy keeping it clean, tidy and safe, too. There's a comfort that comes from routinely eliminating junk, and replacing or fixing things that are broken.

If you can, surround yourself solely with what brings you joy and calm. William Morris, the father of the Arts & Crafts movement, said, 'Have nothing in your house that you do not know to be useful, or believe to be beautiful.' Keeping beauty and order on the outside will support you in feeling peaceful and orderly on the inside. As within, so without, remember?

It's considered wise to be discerning, too, about whom you let into your home; it will help to keep up the positive energy you're building up around you. If you don't like someone's vibe, don't invite them in.

Keep dried white sage handy in your home, to use if ever you feel uncomfortable about someone who's been there, or there's been an argument. Light the sage and ask for yourself and for your place to be cleansed psychically. Allow the smoke to billow around you, and into the rooms of your home. 'Spiritual cleansing rituals for you and your home play an important part in psychic safety and building up your light in general,' says Cher.

39

7. Help others

'We're all here to help each other, aren't we?' to quote a gentleman I overheard on a bus once. We do nothing alone. So, let's give gladly – especially to the vulnerable – expecting nothing in return. Share peacefully your time, skills, knowledge and compassion – and watch yourself get happier. The possibilities for doing good are endless!

8. Have faith

Faith is essential to happiness. Faith in ourselves, faith in others, and above faith all in the Divine. Faith is active; we build faith by showing it.

The wisdom-keepers of history also say that faith comes through listening: when you tune in to the divine voice or vision within, you receive prompts, guidance and instructions. Acting on them with faith and fortitude, as great initiates across the centuries have done, gives you real strength – and power!

To demonstrate real faith is to give yourself to Divine Will regardless of what you think, or want: you'll know a message is from the Divine if it is harmless, selfless and desireless. If not, it's not from the Divine. Try this for yourself?

One of my favourite stories of real faith is that of early 20th-century Spiritual Master Paramahansa Yogananda, whose destiny it was to introduce yoga to the West. Yogananda was in deep meditation at home in east India when he had a vision of a crowd of Americans listening to him intently. The next day he received a letter inviting him to speak at an International Congress of Religious Liberals in America (where he was later to meet in person many of those he'd seen in his vision).

Head all awhirl because he'd never given a speech in English, Yogananda went to his Guru Sri Yukteswar, who declared, 'English or no English, your words on yoga will be heard in the West.' The yogi embarked on a two-month ocean voyage to Boston, on which passengers got to hear of him, and invited him to give a talk.

Yogananda desperately tried to organise his thoughts in English, but failed. Standing resolute before his audience, he sent out a silent prayer for guidance, and heard Sri Yukteswar's voice booming within his consciousness, 'You can! Speak!'

Yogananda then gave a 45-minute lecture in stirring and correct English: a talk he later couldn't recall a word of, but nevertheless won him several invitations to speak in the US. By showing such faith time and again Yogananda realised his very best self – and ultimately secured bliss.

CHAPTER 5
DIET

When it comes to drink and food
Choose wisely, not by mood
(Fruit and veg and seeds
Will help you do good deeds)

A drastic change of diet was suggested in my very first conversations with my Spiritual Teacher. I was already eating mainly vegetarian food because the retreat in which I was living was meat-free, and I wasn't a big drinker (been there, done that, stained the T-shirt). So I was curious to find out what she meant.

In fact, the signs that it was time to change my ways were already loud – literally! – and clear. In a confessional email to Cher I wrote: 'My gosh! I fart and burp all day. I look three months pregnant, and the physical irritation is so strong that it's brought back a chronic urinary tract problem.'

And then it came: the super-sized diet change, along with the instruction to eliminate **all** alcohol, caffeine, sugar, dairy, meat, bread, olives, onions, mushrooms and garlic. I was also to avoid acidic fruit such as white grapes and apples.

But I love my food! And that was the point. I would come to learn that if we over-indulge the body, which is of this world, we risk losing out on spiritual gains. And I was very keen to be a spiritual aspirant, though I knew next to nothing at this point about The Spiritual Path.

'As you progress further on The Spiritual Path,' Cher told me, 'limitation of diet is a must – your body is vibrating at a different frequency and some foods will become almost as a poison to your system.' The result, she added, would be an increased sense of harmony, and protection from whatever might deter me from my path.

This marked what would become a prolonged period of cleansing and purification. Amazingly, my system responded instantly: within hours of me making the commitment the swelling in my stomach subsided.

Soon I began to enjoy a new world of veggie brands such as Quorn, VBites, and Tivall, which made moreish meat-free versions of my favourite comfort foods – burgers, chicken pies, even roast turkey and gravy. Enjoying plant-based alternatives of such old favourites helped me through the weaning process.

Over time, the cravings disappeared, and Earl Grey, milk chocolate and coffee became nothing special. I came to directly experience how the pleasures of the body ultimately do nothing for the spirit, and in rising above the temptation of instant gratification experienced an inner strength that felt a lot like peace. What's more, my chronic IBS vanished without trace.

'If a man aspires towards a righteous life, his first act of abstinence is from injury to animals,' declared Nobel Prize-winning theoretical physicist Albert Einstein. Like most spiritual centres the world over, Osho Risk serves purely vegetarian meals. Delicious it is, too. Yet on the rare occasions that some of us left on a day trip into town we'd gleefully order burgers and hot dogs. (This was before I became a student of The Spiritual Path, of course.)

I've since learned that Osho's recorded thoughts on vegetarianism include:

'Wherever meditation has happened, people have become vegetarian, for thousands of years. Vegetarianism functions as a purification. When you eat animals you are more under the law of necessity. When you are a vegetarian you are lighter and more under the law of grace. Try vegetarianism and you will be surprised: meditation becomes far easier.'

A year or two before being instructed to follow a plant-based diet, I discussed the topic with a friend. For her, there was no difference between eating a pet and eating a cow – a statement to which I reacted strongly. Yet I had no cogent argument – I just disagreed! It is said that of the three stages of truth, the first is ridicule, the second violent opposition, and the third acceptance.

After almost a year of going veggie, and while resting in deep meditation, I saw myself as a tall man in big workmen's boots. A tough farmer type. In one hand I held the fresh carcass of a lamb. With the other I wrung out its guts and blood. Within seconds, I began to feel distressed. Distress turned to regret and I fell to my knees saying sorry to the lamb and its kind for my brutality. In tears, I prayed for forgiveness, strength and guidance.

Then a miracle happened! I watched the lamb come back to life, as perfect as had been before I killed it. As it shook back into life, my whole body in this realm began to tremble strongly. In amazement I asked what would it like? 'Respect me,' replied the lamb.

When I told Cher, she revealed that my being a slaughterman was a past life and that what I'd experienced was an important journey with a deep lesson – because I was ready to learn it. Ready to recognise and address all the suffering I'd caused to one of the most defenceless animals on Earth.

It also meant that I was ready to fully stop being in any way complicit in anything that involved that kind of suffering, not just in this life but any lifetime to come. And this is why I committed to a non-violent lifestyle and became vegan. Try it?

SIX STEPS TO A NON-VIOLENT DIET
1. Eat harmlessly
Meaning no being has had to suffer or die for you to feed your physical vehicle. Both Gandhi and Apple founder Steve Jobs were fruitarian for years.

2. Bless your food
A prayer of thanks also increases the energy vibration of what you're about to consume, which in turn benefits your vitality.

3. Limit treats
Chocolate, pastries, wine, beer and so on are fine in moderation. Fruit, veg and seeds can make great snacks.

4. Share with care
Eating with someone is a symbolically intimate act in which you share more than just a meal. If you're unsure abut the person you're to dine with, consider having just a drink with them.

5. Keep time

Try eating at set times to improve your metabolic rate. The discipline is ennobling, too.

6. Meditate and pray

Ask inwardly for guidance about your eating habits. Prompts may then come in a dream, or meditation, or through an intuition. More than once, I've seen green beans, and lemons appear in meditation – a sign to eat them more. Marni, a friend's delightful young daughter, dreamed of an avocado with a face that talked to her in her tummy. It was literally telling her where to put (more) avocado!

CASE STUDIES
Hair-raising healing

David, an Indian father of two, one of whom is one of my best friends, started losing his hair in his thirties. By his early fifties he'd lost nearly all the hair at the front of his head, and the rest was thinning.

David was a meat eater, and as he also had a sweet tooth, he ate a lot of sugar and fat too. His wife, on the other hand, is a lifelong vegetarian who rarely drinks milk, and never eats eggs. Two years ago David switched to his wife's diet of grains, pulses, vegetables, lots of fruit, and no alcohol. Today, miraculously, his hair has almost all grown back.

Instant transformation

Within a year of starting to meditate regularly, a client of mine, Emma, turned vegetarian in a flash! Resting in bed at the end of the day she knew in an instant, 'I'm vegetarian now.' She then cried for three hours, as if to say goodbye to meat, while also expressing her guilt at having eaten it. It was a surprisingly short process. After the tears and a really deep sleep she woke up in a new state of being, and hasn't looked back.

Natural vegetarian

One of my neighbour's teenage granddaughters has intuitively refused meat since she was a child – even though her family and traditional agricultural community all eat meat. When I last saw them, her mother had bought sausage rolls for tea, the pastry of which the girl was delicately picking and folding in her mouth, the sausage untouched.

Kindly note: the Divine assures me that if a mother is vegetarian, her child is born vegetarian.

Veggie pets

A harmless diet can be successfully extended to cats and dogs. My friend's glossy-coated Chihuahuas are doing extremely well on a 100 percent vegetarian diet, which they've been on since three months old. Another friend's pet, Tom the cat, is – like my Lili – predominantly vegetarian and gets glowing health reports from the vet. The commercial dry food we feed them has all essential foodstuff and nutrients their species' needs, including taurine – which is great.

CHAPTER 6
DREAMS

At rest, at night
Messages of the Light
Are given in plain sight

Dreams are powerful messages – a direct note from your higher self to you, let's say. I consider them gifts, presented by the subconscious to guide us towards balance and betterment.

For years as a girl I suffered a recurring nightmare: a powerful buzzing would fill my ears and send fear racing through me as I lay frozen in bed, helpless to stop the impending horror. To avoid it, I'd regularly resort to sitting on the stairs late at night waiting for my parents to go to bed, comforted by the sounds of the TV coming from under the living-room door.

Twenty years later, although I hadn't told him about my night terrors, a Swiss mystic called Manuel Schoch would ask me if I remembered sleeping badly and hearing sounds when I was five. He could read the imprint of them in my aura, which he described as an electro-magnetic field surrounding my body.

As generous as he was with his insights, Manuel didn't explain what the sounds were, and to this day they remain a mystery to me. I trust the truth will be revealed when I'm ready to know it.

In my very first session as a student of Cher's she instructed me to watch my dreams for three nights and make notes.

On the first night I had nothing clear to report.

On the second, I dreamt I was to make two soups: one garlic and mushroom, one onion. 'Your dream indicates a need for diet changes to assist you in future,' explained Cher. 'Some monks eliminate the above-mentioned foods to aid them in handling and transmuting the sex energy. Food and spirituality are intrinsically linked – hence most communes and retreats being vegetarian or vegan.'

On the third night, I saw the androgynous face of a helper in spirit (I wasn't then aware it was a helper, it was Cher who revealed its identity). As my spiritual training advanced I was to learn that there are distinct types of dreams, and also learn how to decipher – as well as direct – them at will. I'd like to share some examples I've heard or experienced first-hand:

Premonition (romantic relationship)
In her mid 20s, Sarah dreamt of being in a car with someone who offered her their gloved hand to hold as they drove down a street that was wet after the rain. At the time, she was strongly attracted to someone.

Months later he asked her out. Driving her home after their first date, the exact dream scenario played itself out, with the roads wet from the rain and her date putting on driving gloves and offering her his hand.

She felt that this déjà vu was highly significant and meant they were destined to be together. The attraction she felt was very strong, yet their first kiss when he dropped her off left Sarah feeling sick to her stomach. She tried to get over the feeling but never came to be comfortable around him.

A few months later, she attended a seminar about how humans are energy beings, where she learned about psychic attacks and how certain people can cause us to feel unwell. She realised this is exactly how she felt when with her boyfriend, and that the dream was one of warning and not of an impending romance. Thankfully, the day she went to break up with him, he ended the relationship first.

Deity healing

Vivek, a long-term student of Advaita, the Eastern philosophy of non-duality, and a remarkably learned clinician who teaches other clinicians all over the world, once told the story in a class of his brother who'd suffered chronic back pain. The brother had gone to countless medical experts, in more than one country, some of whom were the best in their field. But nothing shifted it.

Then one night, in a dream, a joyful deity visited the brother – one that was specific to the region of India in which he was born. Its presence made him laugh so much that he woke himself. From that day on he was cured!

Prophetic dream (work)

I stepped towards a large window with a young woman, who said, 'I know you agreed to 10%, but we want to give you the 40% you originally asked for.' As she spoke, an air of appreciation and love arose around us.

Just a few days later, a kindly female colleague emailed me:

Hi Maggie,
I've attached details of the sessions you did and outlines of the final amount you should invoice us for. I've kept it at you receiving 40%, as 10% seems way too low – regardless of what we agreed.

Helping dream

The first time I had this type of dream was soon after joining The Spiritual Path. It felt very real; my heart was still pounding even after waking.

I was walking in company down an alley somewhere in the Middle East when I spotted a woman in her 40s lying half-naked on the street floor. Something awful had obviously happened: her breasts were exposed and the atmosphere surrounding her was one of horror. As we approached, she began scrambling on all fours, moving crab-like onto the pavement and into a passageway to the right.

At the same time a black-cloaked figure – his back to us – caught my attention. He seemed to be the perpetrator. The alarm in my group intensified and we rallied to both protect her and catch him as he ran off.

Some followed him as I leant down to the woman, whose deathly-white face was contorted, saying, 'We're with you now.' The blonde lady next to me covered her gently in a pale purple scarf as I reached for a pale pink cardigan to put on her. The vibration of protection was strong.

When I told Cher, she said, 'I am happy you are helping others in the dream state. You need to grow in strength, which is why you felt some fear.'

DECIPHERING YOUR DREAMS: KEY POINTS
Creepy crawlies
Spiders and reptiles are often a warning of some kind.

Pregnancy and babies

Dreams of pregnancy and babies usually symbolise the birth of a new project, or an aspect of yourself that needs attending to.

Recurring dreams

Repetitive dreams are a strong prompt that something needs addressing and acting on.

Water

Water signifies one of two things: emotions, or cleansing. Was the water clear or muddy? The clearer it is, the better.

CHAPTER 7
OVERCOMING NEGATIVITY

Purity of soul is thy goal

Of the many ornaments decorating our home when I was growing up, the one that most intrigued me was called 'See No Evil, Speak No Evil, Hear No Evil', a representation of three brass monkeys whose hands covered, variously, their eyes, mouth and ears. Perhaps my higher self already knew that I was destined to lead a good life and heed their implicit lesson to still my restless 'monkey mind'...

The command to see no evil, speak no evil and hear no evil are part of a monk's training. Shaolin monks, for example, are extremely strict about not allowing negativity into their sphere; if you say or do something offensive they may literally shut their eyes and cover their ears right in front of you.

Why? Because negativity blocks us from the gifts and loving relationships we are meant to experience in this lifetime. Remove the blocks and the blessings can come to you. This is spiritual law.

Negativity is rooted in the lower self, which is selfish. Fear, greed, self-pity are among its foot soldiers, and all distort our light, like dirt on a diamond. I, for one, have a lot of cleaning up to do.

If I'd been born male in this incarnation I'd have been called Frank. For that is what I've been much of my life! I may have been blessed with a lot of sweetness, but what has come out of my mouth over the years has at times been shocking! My untamed words offended friends, family, partners, colleagues, and strangers, and I tended to speak too fast and in harsh tones. From my childhood, my parents also complained that I mumbled.

As an aspirant, I was expected to master my mind and negativity in order to become a better being. As a person's inner power grows, so does the effect of what they emit. The less of the lower self there is, the more the Divine can work through us. This is how Yeshua was able to turn water into wine, for example, and how Saint Valentine returned his jailer's daughter's sight to her. It's also how some Masters can transmute someone deserving's karma for them.

As I continued with my spiritual practices, making a conscious effort not to swear, complain or let anything rash, unkind, or rooted in anger come out of my lips, my speech began to both soften and slow down. I even began to be complimented on the calming effect of my voice. 'I can't explain how, but your voice is just so special, Maggie,' said one friend, touchingly.

But the battle wasn't won. As I drew close to reaching the halfway point of my spiritual training there was an unexpected turn in my daily mental activity. Out of the blue, my lower self started blaspheming – frequently – as I went about my day.

Not out loud but in my thoughts. It would swear about anybody, from my devotional flatmate to my cat, to me and even, at the very lowest point, to my Teacher. It would tend to be more activated on public transport: I'd stand there inwardly wincing and outwardly blinking as my lower mind lobbed an insult, which could be several times a minute.

Later, the word bombs became sexual. 'Cock sucker,' my

lower mind would inwardly say when passing a man – any man! – in the street. My negativity was indiscriminate in its base attacks.

Cher explained that the genital references were sex energy, because I still hadn't decided which way I was ultimately to go on The Path: the family way or the celibate way. 'Karmic things play on your psyche until they're forgiven by the Divine and yourself,' she helpfully explained.

After that conversation, my counter-attack plan became three-fold: pray for forgiveness daily, and also every time I caught myself blaspheming, and read a specific prayer as much as possible.

'I want to have sex with you.'
Please forgive me.

'Stupid bitch'
Please forgive me.

If someone could have heard the soundtrack inside my head they'd have thought I was mad! But I was willing to do whatever it took to win the war being waged within me.

All this effort wasn't going unnoticed. Kate, a good friend, wrote to me hesitantly around this time, saying that she'd had a dream about me passing away. 'It felt very real, but the feeling wasn't horrid, it was really peaceful.' Her dream indicated that she'd recognised psychically that my old self and old ways had begun to die away, and that she'd felt the peace that ultimately comes from such a process.

My efforts were also rewarded with prompts to take actions

that would quicken my purification process. One morning as I woke I saw the name Poseidon appear in my mind's eye. (Poseidon is the Greek god of the ocean.)

Then, while waiting for a train at Green Park Tube station 1 four days later, I was astonished to see a young man in a fashionable jacket emblazoned with *Galwad y Môr* – meaning the call of the sea in Welsh! Seeing any words in my mother tongue is rare.

Water both cleanses and heals, and as I'd learned by now to take spiritual prompts seriously, I organised a trip to visit my friend Sachi in the coastal town of Brighton, where we enjoyed an uplifting time.

Some weeks later, by Divine grace and some head-chopping inner journeys, I eventually succeeded in my mental mission: the negative phrases stopped and my equilibrium was restored. Hurray! (I have not yet transcended my lower self, however – the rude inner monologue occasionally resurfaces.)

Negativity is rooted in free will; our moment-to-moment decisions. To free ourselves from the binds that stop us from being who we long to be, we must transmute it. If it isn't transformed into a positive flow of pure energy, the negativity we put out may return to us in one form or another; one life or another.

I learned this the hard, yet ultimately gratifying, way one winter. I was enjoying myself on a night out with friends, including an acquaintance who'd in the past provoked me with disrespectful comments about my open-minded way of life.

Noticing cold-like feelings in my chest, I went home early, and once there developed a fierce fever, which it took me five weeks to recover from. (On the rare occasions I'm poorly, it usually lasts for a few days, maximum.) Before joining The Path, I would have taken my illness at face value, but now I looked more deeply into the cause of my symptoms. In meditation I was shown the man I'd been speaking to, and understood how his feelings about me had unwittingly crystallised into a psychic attack.

I was also shown a past life together in which we'd indulged our lower selves. Shocking as this was, it helped me better understand why he acted that way around me at times, and showed me why I needed to keep my distance from now on.

'Have you got to the root of your emotions?' Cher asked once, referring to my recurring anger and frustration about a certain relationship. 'Emotions cause us stress. If you had a pain in your arm, you'd look to see where the pain was focused. It's the same when dealing with emotions: you need to find their focus so that you can transmute them. Then you gain power.'

HOW TO OVERCOME NEGATIVITY

As well as prayer, meditation and being kind, peaceful and positive, here are other practical ways to triumph over the 'heavy' darkness of the lower self:

1. Face your fears

What we avoid in fear grows in power over us the longer we hide from it. A great deal of unnecessary suffering can be avoided by nipping negative feelings in the bud. That way they don't get a chance to steal your light.

In meditation, focus your mind on the part of your body in which the emotion(s) 'live'. Use your mind to go into the energy vortex here and watch quietly to see what may be revealed to you – visual scenes, or audible clues or words of guidance, for instance. Don't try to change anything you see, but stay focused and neutral while humbly asking to be healed. Close by giving thanks to the Divine.

2. Release the wrongs

Rituals to release your fears will help you to balance yourself and transmute bad karma. This is Cher's advice: tear a sheet of white paper into strips and allow your negative thoughts and feelings about yourself and others to emerge. Write each thought or feeling on a strip, and when you've 'emptied' your negativity onto the strips, ask for healing to take place. Then burn the papers.

3. Nip negative thoughts in the bud

As soon as you catch a negative thought forming, throw it out. Stop it before it forms a sentence, and replace it with a positive thought or a humble request for forgiveness. Or you can mentally start playing the title and main chorus of The Supremes' classic, *Stop! In the Name of Love*. It will at the very least make you smile!

When you feel a negative thought bubbling up, do whatever it takes to stop it coming out and creating bad karma. Cover your mouth, make an excuse to leave the room, laugh out loud – experiment to see what works for you.

4. Pray for strength

Humbly ask the Divine to grant you the strength to overcome your negativity. Be confident in your ability to achieve your goal. With the Divine, everything is possible.

5. Direct the flow

If you find the person you're speaking with becoming increasingly negative, you're not helping them – or yourself – by letting them ramble on. If they're speaking unkindly about themselves or another, try lightly saying, 'Well, we all have our weaknesses, don't we?' or 'I'm capable of worse.' That's likely to stop them in their tracks.

6. Keep good company

Keeping the company of good, positive people – ideally those making the same efforts as you – is vital. If, however, almost everyone you know is negative, this is a reflection of your inner state, and it's best not to pass judgement. Instead, focus on creating your own happiness.

7. Be grateful

Feeling and expressing thanks continually will help prevent negativity from taking away your light and making you unhappy, listless or frustrated. True self-betterment comes when we're thankful *even* when things aren't unfolding as we'd like them to. There is always a reason to be grateful, for the Divine is always with us, guiding our path.

CHAPTER 8
FORGIVENESS

Forgiveness comes from up above
To help us learn how to love

'Forgiveness is everything.' Many, many times have I clairaudiently heard the Divine say this. So what *is* forgiveness? What are its roots and possibilities?

It is written that if we do not forgive, we cannot go to the Divine. Until we truly forgive, we cannot go all the way on the road of self-betterment. Because until we truly forgive, we cannot truly heal.

How can a person take the life of another, for example, and it not be right to repent? Do we give life? As some of my past lives were revealed to me, regret at the harm I have caused has flooded through my heart and being. Surely remorse and the upwelling wish to atone is a universal impulse? A timeless prompt to balance the scales of karma?

Most of us know what it is to hold a grudge or worse. It weighs heavily, colouring our thoughts with suffering, keeping us rigid in the name of self-righteousness. Yet the other person's deed is done. We've survived, and endless possibilities for healing, growth and happiness remain open to us.

So I wonder what good, if any, is there in staying stuck? In what way does it serve to continue to pay such a heavy price; one that's possibly as – or more – damaging than the original offence? If we remain fixed in our thinking, we ourselves stop our wondrous trajectory and miss out on life's gifts. Wouldn't it be better to be light and agile, like a butterfly in flight?

'A man who bows down to nothing can never bear the burden of himself,' warned 19th-century Russian novelist Fyodor Dostoyevsky. You literally see it in the bodies of some people; presumably weighed down and almost bent double by the burden of not having forgiven those who've wronged them, nor having atoned for their own unkindly deeds.

Until I became an aspirant, forgiving myself and others wasn't something I'd consciously considered, yet now I'm so grateful for this life-changing practice. Without fail, every time I focus deeply on forgiveness I feel a renewal of peace and strength in my innermost heart. Difficult feelings of emotional weakness melt away and I am lifted. The boat stops rocking.

If the past keeps haunting you, start forgiving. It doesn't mean saying that what the person did was OK. It does mean setting yourself free and triggering a higher law that creates potential miracles on your path.

It is a miracle to me that I can meet my childhood abuser and shake his hand, feeling compassion for him as a fellow human being with his own cross to bear, just like me. Just like you.

We are all equal in being imperfect, and that truth is freeing! When all is said and done, we each have virtues and we each have darkness, so who are we to judge? This truth frees me to express that there are many, many things for which I have sought – and continue to seek – forgiveness.

When I was at the right point in my training, Cher suggested that, before going into silent prayers and meditation every night, I ask for anything and everything I may have done, said or thought at any time to offend anyone to be revealed to me.

Essentially I'd be asking for assistance in cleaning the slate of my subconscious, which was inevitably going to trigger visions and nightmares and a lot of emotion. As my offences were revealed, I was to ask for forgiveness. 'It's the only way to transmute these energies,' she explained.

One night, I inwardly found myself on a battlefield of corpses. The fighting hadn't long ended, and I was sad. Sad at all the loss. Sad at being a 'good' killer, when deep inside I had a compassionate heart, and felt tired, so tired of all the fighting and death. I went around pulling out swords from bodies, gathering them beneath my arm to reuse. But then I stopped and pulled off a white undergarment from beneath my armour to lay on the ground in offering to the Divine.

Cher explained: 'Past lives are etched in our psyche. Transmute them by praying for forgiveness in this life. For the beginnings of Inner Work this is required. Then one can travel higher.'

Whenever we're negative in thought, word or action, whether we're complaining, cruel, irresponsible, greedy, etc., we're causing harm – and adding to the forces of darkness in the world. With each offence, we put up a barrier on the road between us and "Home", the Divine. Yet each time we sincerely ask for forgiveness, that block can be lifted, bringing us closer to blissful union again.

HOW TO FORGIVE

Forgiving and seeking forgiveness as we go is like washing our karmic saucepan straight after using it: the 'dirt' tends to wash off easily. But let the pan sit a while and you'll have to scrub it to get it clean. The work will take longer and require more effort.

For many, anger builds a stubborn, disfiguring crud over their joy and inner peace. It may be that you first need to face your rage in a safe and conscious way before being able to access the lighter vibrations of (self) compassion and forgiveness. SE sessions with a certified practitioner, and prayer, as well as the exercises below, can all help tremendously.

Ask for forgiveness

Whenever you catch yourself doing anything to harm or offend another, try to stop yourself and – ideally there and then – apologise by saying, 'Please forgive me (for)...' and naming the offending behaviour.

For example, much to my chagrin (I really should have overcome this by now!) I still get impatient with my mother. Yet when I've found the right moment I'll gently say, 'Forgive me for being short with you earlier.' 'It's alright,' she usually responds, and we go back to enjoying our day.

The law of forgiveness will still be set in motion if you can't apologise in person, but do so by email, text or over the phone. Remember, you can be right or you can be happy!

Pray for forgiveness

Close your eyes and still your mind as best you can. Direct your focus on – or better *inside* – your heart centre and the energy vortex there. Now direct your thoughts upwards to the Divine, and pray for forgiveness for your own negative thoughts, and your unkind words and actions. Pray from your heart so that you can transmute negative forces into a healing flow of positive energy.

Keep forgiveness lists
Keep two lists. The first, of all the people you need to forgive (including yourself), and why. The second of all the things you've said, done, or thought that you wish to seek forgiveness for. Be as specific as possible. Excel sheets works well for this practice, if you're an Excel kind of person (or willing to be). For the most powerful results, keep adding to your lists daily.

For the full and original text on forgiveness lists, see *The Hidden Truths of a Modern Seer*, best read after the first in Cher Chevalier's trilogy, *The Hidden Secrets of a Modern Seer*.

When a person is making a sincere effort, they will be helped to better themselves. Within a fortnight of starting his forgiveness lists, Paul, a meditation client of mine and a very successful lawyer, found himself while at work in his office being compelled to grab a sheet of paper and write down a fresh list of things for which he needed forgiveness.

Forgiveness builds a ladder to heaven here on Earth. When we bless another, we ourselves are blessed.

CASE STUDIES
Struggle to forgive an ex
Two years into my training I began dating a kindly entrepreneur named Carl. The more time we spent together,

the more acutely aware I became of the weaknesses in me that needed transmuting – mainly lack of compassion, and cruelty in speech.

Though Carl could be loving, he was by nature slothful, would eat meat in front of me, and focused most of his attention on making money and building an easy life for himself. Reminded that finding a spiritual man is like finding a needle in a haystack, and that there was a higher purpose to our relationship, I fought to the point of exhaustion to keep things light between us. Despite our best efforts to tolerate our differences, after seven months they proved too stark and the relationship sadly ended.

Life and my spiritual unfoldment continued and I thought all was well, until Cher decreed that I needed to forgive Carl FULLY for disrespecting me. 'If you have anything against anyone, you can't go to the Divine,' she said. 'When you can, real joy comes within you.'

I listened in silence, chastened.

'He didn't rob or kill you. Put it in perspective, Maggie. Seeing it from this perspective will extend your tolerance and patience. It was an opportunity for both of you to grow and for you to help him become more harmless in life. But he just wasn't ready. The Divine will want to see how you respond when someone hurts you.'

Humbled, I vowed to focus on forgiving my fellow pilgrim completely. Not long after, in the dream state, we met in a café in a public square. I offered him a plate of vegetarian sushi, told him he had a good heart and as I got up to leave his table, kissed him affectionately.

'Offering food shows you wish him well,' revealed Cher. 'Unconditional love is the kiss on head. You're free now.'

Murderous child

Stepping into my kitchen from the lounge to get a glass of water for a client, I heard, 'Murderous child!' sound in my mind. I caught my breath. Me?!

Two hours later, while walking to Hampstead Heath, the phrase resounded again in my mind. Paying attention this time, a familiar childhood scene of an outside wall of my Pembrokeshire primary school appeared in my inner vision. I was in the schoolyard looking at an unpainted cement windowsill on which tens of tiny blood spiders (as we called them) were crawling. I was squishing them with my little fingers – something I actually did as a child.

Horrified, the adult me began praying fervently for forgiveness, clear now that the red spider mites were doing nothing to harm me and had as much right to be there as me. The Divine responded, 'Until one is holy, one cannot step in the footsteps of the gods.'

CHAPTER 9
LOSING A LOVED ONE

The ties of love are never broken
Do not let sorrow be outspoken

'I've got some bad news, Mags... Dad's dead.'

Two words. One shattering blow. Everything looked the same – the London sky, trees, buildings, cars, people – but the world as I'd known it for 38 years had fundamentally changed in an instant. I wanted to wail, 'Why are you going about your day as if nothing's happened? My dad's *died!*'

My father passed peacefully on a sunny walk in nature the day after his 79th birthday, on 9 June 2014. He left behind 55 years of happy marriage, three children, three grandchildren, three great grandchildren and a legacy of wisdom, wit, love, and a collection of chocolate bar wrappers stuffed down the side of the sofa.

Dad had been selfless, moral and generous his entire adult life, and I never once heard him speak badly of anyone. Whatever the right thing to do was, dad would do it – regardless of any inconvenience to himself – and he never once sought thanks or praise for his quiet efforts to do good. Doing the right thing included admitting that he'd done me wrong by not talking to me fully about the sexual abuses I'd suffered.

Our families are our strongest karmic ties, and I cannot reduce to words how powerful the bond was between my father and me. Only Cher understood. My dad's passing may have all been too much for me if she hadn't warned me of it three years previously. As unsettling as it was, being told of dad's passing in advance was a great blessing. It gave me time to polish up my relationship with all of my family, and encourage everyone to rebuild any broken bridges between them and dad.

Communication was easier between us, and I became closer to everyone. Dad and I became more affectionate in those final years, as the rough edges of our differing ways of expressing love were smoothed. I say more affectionate; in fact, it was in this healing phase that I taught him how to hug!

The first time I asked him for a hug as an adult was in 2011 when standing at the bottom of the stairs of our family home, with him a few feet away in the lounge. 'If I must,' he quipped as we embraced. I felt giddy with happiness.

These magical moments of harmony would grow over the coming years and meant that the last thing we did together in this realm – though we didn't know it at the time – was hug. A big, slightly shy, unhurried hug in which pure love emanated in mutual blessing.

Almost as soon as I arrived in Wales after the news of dad's passing, my family began focusing on doing things exactly as he would have wished them done. I was told this was very important. Fortunately, with him being such a strong character, it was easy and decisions were soon agreed on.

He wanted, for example, to be buried in a remote rural church on the opposite side of the valley from my beautiful childhood home; a house he'd largely built himself. Reached by a narrow winding track, flanked by mature native trees, it's a wonderfully peaceful spot, especially on a bright summer's day like the one of the funeral.

We enjoyed the eulogies immensely and by the time the moment for the final one had come, I felt strengthened. Standing to face the crammed-in crowd, I honoured dad's exceptional existence in a few paragraphs, one of which quoted the most important book of his life, *Meditations* by Roman Emperor and Stoic philosopher Marcus Aurelius. It sums up the great soul that in this lifetime I'm honoured to call 'dad', and offers timeworn guidance for us all:

'Keep yourself simple, good, pure, serious, and unassuming; the friend of justice and godliness; kindly, affectionate, and resolute in your devotion to duty. Strive your hardest to be always such a man as Philosophy would have you to be.

Reverence the gods, succour your fellow mortals. Life is short, and this earthly existence has but a single fruit to yield – holiness within, and selfless action without...

Scorn notoriety, be industrious and patient; master the facts, suffer unjust criticisms without replying in kind. Be no friend to talebearers. Remember all this, so that when your own last hour comes your conscience may be clear.'

The eulogy ended with the congregation resting in some minutes' silence as we focused on wishing dad well on his journey through eternity. Everyone agreed it was a really lovely funeral.

Back in London the following week, my friend Gina invited

me to hers to do yoga. During the meditation at the end I sensed a wave of light and love wash over me, evoking tears of relief. Later, Gina – who'd also developed psychic abilities, the potential for which I believe everyone shares – told me that my dad had been kneeling at my side, his hand on my head. (I would, in coming months, again sense him place his hand there as I inwardly heard 'Bendith'– Welsh for blessing.)

Afterwards, I cried by myself for an hour on the garden patio, comforted by the trees and air. Some moments I laughed, and others I anguished, wishing with all my breaking heart that I could have said goodbye. As the tissues piled up beside me on the sofa, a delightful little wren captured my attention. It came and danced on the ground before its audience of one, joyfully hoping from one side of the large patio to the other.

As the weeks went by I began to feel less exhausted and more stable. But still a thin black layer of grief lay over me. To help me through, Cher explained that a parent has a very strong urge to guide their offspring and loved ones back on Earth after passing. Quite often they give clear and strict instructions.

Dad had three concise messages to impart, I discovered, sobbing as I wrote them down. 'There are very loving minds behind you,' said Cher softly as we ended our call, leaving me deeply comforted.

As natural as it is to grieve, a student of The Spiritual Path is expected to not dwell on negative feelings but stay focused on being peaceful and cheerful. Two months after dad had passed, I decided to lift my spirits with a walk to Primrose Hill, where poet William Blake in a vision saw the 'Spiritual Sun'.

As I lay relaxing on the warm grass, to my amazement an energy introduced itself claircognisantly as the spirit of Primrose Hill. Aware that my visitor was communicating to help me, I listened with an open heart: 'Be wise, little one. Be quiet of mind and peaceful of heart. Thou cryest for nothing. Celebrate union!'

Feeling uplifted, I pondered the meaning of union in this context. Was it about everything true in life being eternal and therefore unbreakable? A couple of months later things would become much clearer.

In a dream, dad walked up to me wearing his familiar navy V-neck jumper, triggering a profound realisation that his essence - his spirit – was still alive. I think I even exclaimed in the dream, 'Oh, you're not dead!' The whole scene can't have lasted much more than a minute. Wherever he is, I know my dad is well.

It was a sign that I was beginning to function from a higher level of consciousness. The spirit – the divine spark within us – is eternal and never dies. The body, something of a machine that we borrow and inhabit for our trip to Earth, by contrast, does. It is temporary, and while it's important to care for it in gratitude, thinking of it is as who we are may only keep us stuck in the pain of separation, which says when someone dies we've lost them forever.

It seems to me that death is simply an end (of the physical body), not *the* end. True life – the eternal, non-physical life of Spirit – is limitless, with no beginning and no end, hence everything being One: unity.

Some liken death to simply moving into the next room; we're all still in the same home, it's just that the individual who's passed has moved to a different space within it. Sometimes, when we're very relaxed, such as when asleep or meditating, we may "slip" through a wall and talk to our loved one again. It's a comforting thought, isn't it?

HOW TO PREPARE A LOVED ONE FOR DEATH

Our parents are our passageway to this realm. How we treat them can directly advance or delay our evolutionary journey – and theirs. We have everything to gain by doing our very best to honour them.

1. Help right wrongs

Where appropriate, gently encourage your loved on to lift their spirit by acting on any regrets or wrongdoings, and asking for forgiveness – where possible from the other person, as well as from the Divine. Equally, if they've been hurt and still hold a grudge against someone, encourage them to forgive them. Whatever they don't address before leaving may only weigh them down.

2. Clear the air

If there's something you've been holding back – positive or negative – clear the air with kindness, choosing your time, and being honest. Encourage other family members to do the same. It will help you, too, not just your loved one. Missing your opportunity to say what needs to be said can be devastating. *Carpe diem!*

3. Tie up loose ends

Helping them get all their affairs in order is important if they're not to leave their tail behind, so to speak. Writing a will is key. If there are debts, get them paid. Also, is there anything they wish to do before they go? What would lift their spirits? Pay attention, be interested and help make those things happen.

4. Explore the unknown

What are your loved one's thoughts about death and the afterlife? Getting them thinking and talking about this should begin to neutralise any fears and ease their passage back to the realms of Spirit. If their understanding is narrow, give hints in an effort to widen it, read spiritual literature to them, or perhaps suggest watching a spiritual film together, such as *Hereafter* starring Matt Damon.

5. Bring peace

Peace is a gateway to eternity. The more peaceful they are when the time comes to pass, the easier and safer will be their passage 'back' into the non-physical realms. Take them to sit or walk in nature, practice sitting in tranquil silence together, ask them to talk about what brings them peace, or play their favourite peaceful music frequently.

ONCE THEY'VE PASSED

1. Pray for them

Pray that your loved one be given safe passage. I was very fortunate in having Cher confirm that dad had crossed into Spirit safely. Not all do. Prayers help. As does sending them light and loving thoughts as you go about your day, just as it would if they were still incarnate.

2. Do things their way

It's been made very clear to me that relatives are to do their best to organise the funeral exactly as the person would have wished it. If your loved one left instructions, follow them precisely. The funeral is the last opportunity to celebrate the person's life and therefore very significant indeed. Should disputes arise, do your best to stay calm and focused on what the person would have wanted.

3. Await their messages

On leaving this realm or even just before, people often have strong prompts to pass on a message to their loved ones. It could be helpful to sit, settle your mind, and focus on the person. Acting on their messages will help bring you peace. Alternatively, seek the assistance of a reputable psychic or medium.

4. Keep something close

If the person you've lost is very dear to you, it can be helpful to keep something of theirs that they used a lot – a pen or keying, for example – on you or near you. It will give you comfort.

5. Continue communicating

The loss from a death comes as a shock, yet psychic ties are not severed that swiftly, so if there's something you need to say to your loved one, talk to them in your mind or even out loud. It will help ease the grieving process and keep the creative channels of love clear.

CASE STUDIES
Husband and wife reunion blessing

Four months had passed since dad had left his body when, in my inner vision, a small being with beautiful big wings led me towards a bright light. Then I heard, 'Thy father is in heaven and doing well. Your mother will join him. She is a good woman.' I burst into tears! So did mam when I told her.

Granted wish dismissed

I got chatting to a member of staff in my local supermarket one evening when the conversation turned to our fathers. After 15 years, he still missed his, he said. He wished to speak to him. He then revealed that he often saw him in his dreams. "Do you talk?" I asked. "Yeah!" he said, with a big smile. "We have chats and fun."

So his wish was already being granted! He was dismissing the blessing – and was chronically angry – because it wasn't happening in the physical world.

Cancer death blessing

I co-host yoga and meditation workshops and on this particular day I had guided the group through a tantric heart meditation. It's a simple, still and silent meditation done in pairs in which each partner takes it in turn to gently hold a hand each side of the other's heart.

A participant, fiercely bright and philosophical by nature, admitted later she'd been dreading it all day. Yet she found the actual experience very positive; she felt that she connected to herself more than she had in a long time. In her own words:

'I learned that trying to understand what's in your heart through the power of rational thought is not the only, nor the best way. Sometimes emotions are non-intentional – that is, they don't have an object. Just to experience them is enough to be able to move on.

I also had a very powerful image of my father during the meditation. He died 10 years ago of cancer, and I can't really picture what he looked like before his illness, unless I have a photograph. I saw him clearly, in full health, laughing!'

Chapter 10
Prayer

The upwelling of the heart
Is an ideal place to start

My earliest experience of prayer was repeating *The Lord's Prayer* in church on Sundays.

Back at home, I loved to 'starfish' on the daisy-speckled grass of our vegetable garden, the bright sunshine pouring down so generously on me that its warmth embraced my small body even from the ground up.

The generous song of swifts and sparrows filled the air, as butterflies dressed in whites, blues, browns, oranges and purples danced jauntily around me. Existence and I were best friends. I see now that I was in a state of what I these days consider prayer; a silent communion with the divine forces of nature, not asking or wanting for anything.

Which do you think was real prayer? Church or outdoors?

I'm not suggesting that ritualised prayers don't have their place on a road to self-betterment. In fact, I still on occasion spontaneously recite *The Lord's Prayer*. What I am suggesting is that prayer is an intimate, very personal contact with our Creator. At times it may even be a beseeching.

Though to date my deepest experience of prayer has been alone at home, I'm as likely to offer a prayer of thanks walking down the street, for the beauty of flowers the sun on my face, or the laughter of a child, for example. As I wrote this chapter I was given the words:

Pray to Me anywhere
For I am with you everywhere.

Beautiful.

On rare occasions, I've entered a spontaneous state of prayer; intoxicated with love or gratitude for the Divine. And there have been other times when I've very consciously bent down on my knees – even in the toilets of the office I was freelancing in, as they were the only private spaces available – begging inwardly for strength to battle my lower self.

If ever you find yourself struggling to pray, it can help tremendously to kneel. When I do, I tend to feel much closer to my Creator and get a much better result. Once I knelt for so long that when I got up I took two comedic steps and fell to the floor, as I couldn't actually feel my legs!

Praying for others is an essential daily practice if we are to better ourselves. For who knows who may be praying for us? I can sense it when particular friends pray for me. Feeling heavy after my dad's passing, I was doing my makeup one morning when I felt a gentle wave of peace wash over me. It was lovely! A few minutes later my WhatsApp pinged; it was a fellow pilgrim on The Path saying she'd been sending me peace.

The all-powerful, all-knowing Divine knows exactly what you, or the person you're praying for needs, thus lists of requests are – happily – redundant. For the best result, I find that praying for Divine Will works excellently.

Real prayer, then, doesn't consist of many words, but instead lies in the thankfulness of the heart. It is in the silence of a kind heart that the Divine hears – and answers – us. The blessings of love can be bestowed on the interior in prayer and meditation.

I've heard claims that meditation and prayer are the same. To be clear, prayer is talking to the Divine – attuning your pure thoughts or loving silence with your Creator. Meditation is listening to the Divine – going deep into your interior to ultimately meet the Divine within you. Two distinct 'movements' and cornerstones of a spiritual life.

CASE STUDIES
Granddaughter healing
Standing outside a meditation class one day, I got chatting to three amiable generations of one family. The grandmother bent her knee and began telling the story of when she suffered chronic knee pain. The pain was particularly bad one day when she was with her granddaughter, and she'd said as much as she went into the bathroom.

When she came out a few minutes later she was amazed to find she had no pain at all! The granddaughter smiled and revealed, 'I sent a prayer for your knees to get better, grandma.' The positive effects of the young girl's loving request lasted quite some time.

Spiritual transformation
Lisa, a devoted mother, prayed for her daughter to turn vegetarian like her, aware that to continue eating meat would be detrimental to her child's karma. Within months, Pearl became a vegetarian, and she's now a passionate advocate for animal rights among her school friends.

Saved from the brink

My friend Lina had shared her concerns with me about a teenage member of her family who'd been self-harming and was extremely distraught. I asked for the girl's date of birth and passed it to Cher, and we both began praying for her.

Some weeks later, the girl's boyfriend ended their relationship. Feeling sad and vulnerable, she went to sit on a bench on the bridge of her hometown. Soon she was joined by a gentleman who asked if she was ok. Gently he took her hand and said, 'Whatever it is, it will pass. Let go of it; it's no good to you.' Then he smiled and left.

From that day the girl made a conscious decision to change. She stopped cutting herself, joined a dance group, and began avoiding the bad crowd she'd hanging around with. Was the gentleman a divine messenger?

CHAPTER 11
FINDING AND WORKING WITH A SPIRITUAL TEACHER

Forged in light
Our bond brings might
To the holy fight

When the student is ready, the Teacher appears. I'd come across this aphorism in my 20s, never once thinking the timeless truth would transform my life, aged 34.

My Spiritual Teacher first appeared in my email inbox four months after I left my London life to live in Osho Risk in Denmark. In her first email to me, Cher introduced her new book about being a disciple on The Spiritual Path. Enthralled by her extreme physic and paranormal experiences, I wrote about them for *Spirit & Destiny* magazine.

Curious that a psychic whose work was rooted in a devotional life and who sounded so lovely and 'normal' had turned up in my life, I requested a personal session. Little did I know that it would herald the start of an exceptional seven-year spiritual training; three and a half years to break the lower self, and a further three and a half years to fully transmute the darkness within into light.

Everything Cher revealed on that first private call ignited my innermost self; the same one that from birth knew that I'm a tourist here, and that things aren't how most people think they are. I very much liked the way she spoke plainly and with authority:

'You've waited a long time for this,' she said. 'You're at the most powerful juncture in your life so far and have the opportunity to really go very deep. As long as your fear doesn't get in your way.' This sent an almost unbearable thrill racing through my being. I didn't know what she meant, only that every part of me was declaring 'YES! Let's go!'

The first step was to be tested. And Cher said it was going to be:

- painful
- frustrating, and
- frightening.

Uh oh. I'd thought the days of facing my shadow in intensive therapy groups and one-to-one sessions was over.

The first test came within days. I was enjoying a walk home along the main road that passes nearby Osho Risk when I noticed a Ford Fiesta-type car speeding right at me on the wrong side of the road. In an instant my awareness expanded to unite with what some call cosmic consciousness, far beyond the limits of self-awareness, in which belief transforms into knowing. Suddenly, I knew that:

- the driver was deliberately trying to scare me
- he wasn't going to go through with ploughing into me.

Sure enough, in the very last few seconds before he'd have hit me, the young male driver swerved sharply out of my way.

I felt freaked – if delighted to be alive! – but didn't tell anyone. Who'd believe me? It was to Cher I turned with relief and gratitude. 'The car scenario was indeed a test,' she wrote in an email. 'Not only of your fear threshold but also of your balance – one must try and temper fear with reason. One must be spiritual *and* practical in this realm if one is to succeed!'

It was clear that Cher had a powerfully incisive overview of everything that was happening to me on every level. I soon came to realise that I could tell her anything, and she'd not only understand, she'd help *me* understand the meaning of my experiences.

It actually felt like a relief to have none of me hidden, for love has nothing to hide. A part of me could have felt lonely in not telling friends about the extraordinary experiences I was having, yet in reality, it felt important and strengthening to stay silent, and to share my hidden secrets with Cher alone.

There would come times when what was seen in my soul was far from spiritual–envy, frustration, vanity, to name a few vices. And at times I'd be embarrassed about revealing the truth, but would do so anyway, such was my trust in Cher. That, and the gradual realisation that she already knew! Modesty is one of her many virtues.

We'd been emailing and speaking over the phone for four months when it was time for us to meet in person. On a winter's day in London, I nervous-excitedly greeted my beautiful Teacher at her home, holding a card I'd made her, and keenly aware that she had great powers that I did not!

By the time we next met, a month later, I'd moved back to London to begin a new chapter, full of hope and excitement now that I was being guided so beautifully and receiving hints about my future. Interestingly, I felt more like we were equals that second time. She even commented on how calm I was. As I went to leave, feeling empowered and nourished in spirit, Cher said, 'In six months' time you're going to be quite a powerhouse.'

In these early months I clung to her almost like a child to its mother. Many magical things were happening to me and it was still solely to Cher I that turned to talk about them. I knew no-one else in my situation.

Graciously, she encouraged me to ask her questions, unfailingly answering each with fascinating facts, teachings and hints, while reminding me of the importance of continuing with my practices. I felt so uplifted whenever she congratulated me or called me pretty little M!

The intense 'just the two of us' phase began to wane after Cher organised a dinner for a small group of her students at a Michelin-starred vegetarian restaurant. It was a happy evening and a sign of blessings to come. I felt very privileged to be mixing in such circles, making beautiful new friends who also led devotional lives and were strict vegetarians – and with whom I could discuss my esoteric experiences in confidence. (I was still keeping my spiritual experiences secret from my other friends and my family.)

This shift in whom I socialised with reflected a change in my relationship with Cher. We now began meeting in the inner realms, too. At least, I began to become aware of us meeting there. In one sublime dream I saw us bathed in a gentle golden light, united hand in hand in an omnipresent peace as we walked meditatively across a field towards Home, symbolised by my childhood home.

When going about my day, I'd often sense her protective energy surrounding me, and would sometimes feel the love of her prayers soothing my psyche. The ineffable power of the invisible is evident all the time, should we care to think about it deeply. Gravity, air, music, electricity, fragrance – all are extremely powerful forces that you can't see. They can touch you. But can you touch them?

I realised that all my life my dad had been teaching me the same lesson that Cher now was. Only once did he say, 'I love you,' and that was when he was coming round from anaesthetic. But he'd *shown* his love every day – giving me his time, playing games with me, teaching me, encouraging me to work hard, and think of others... Both Cher and dad were as immoveable as a mountain where principles were concerned, and as fluid as a river in adapting their wisdom to suit who they were talking to.

Also, like dad, Cher encouraged me to read. As I devoured the mind-blowing, heart-opening sacred literature she recommended, I began to better understand the relationship between Spiritual Teacher and student. The bond is eternal and cannot be broken, while each has a duty to assist each another (something I wish I'd done much more of. Foolishly I thought that Cher didn't need my prayers or assistance because she was so evolved. I was wrong).

If life was a hill, I'd at least realised by my early 30s that at the top was blissful, unconditional love that was not like fallible human love at all. Yet, because of my level of awareness, I was nevertheless stuck going round and round the hill, taking the long way to the top, and still, unbeknown to me, building up darkness that could undo any progress and send me sliding downwards – as if I'd landed on a snake in a game of Snakes & Ladders.

I was still too focused on myself and my wants, and knew next to nothing about Divine Will and mankind's relationship to it. The quiet arrival of Cher lifted me off that circuitous route and placed me on a direct path straight up the hill to The Absolute. Many, many times she'd encourage me with these magic words: 'I'm behind you.' And, much to my joyous delight, she once wrote: 'The Spiritual PATH is not for the faint of heart but for the seekers of GLORY. The DIVINE is the goal! :) You are on your way!'

It is a privilege to be given the strength to lead a spiritual life. And I was expected to honour what I was being given by sustaining my inner strength through daily spiritual practices, including showing active faith. Faith that what I was being told was truth, for example.

In the early days, some of Cher's teachings clashed with those that I'd come to believe. Yet, under her protection, I was to have hidden truths revealed to me about the body and sex energy, and their relationship to karma and the soul. In return, and out of respect, I was expected to do as I was instructed, be responsible, and work hard every day to overcome my lower self. To pass the tests and forge ahead to the goal of self-betterment – and ultimately Self-Mastery – demands total obedience.

I realised that the stronger my emotional reaction to an instruction, the more I needed to obey it. This is because the lower self has no interest in spiritual work; in the greater good, if you like. It is interested solely in an easy life in which it pleases itself. That is why an aspirant is expected to pray for Divine Will, and forget their own will.

'If they become complacent they won't lose the light, but they'll stay at that point,' warned Cher. Once, when I asked how she was, she said, 'Happy dancing to the Divine's tune!' That still makes me smile.

Through all of my training, all of the ups and downs, Cher was a paragon of purity, virtue, and kindness, as well as an endless fountain of exact sacred knowledge. She could be strict and admonishing when needed, but mainly she advised, guided, warned and encouraged me with infinite patience and compassion. 'I'm praying for you every day, don't you worry,' she said one day. I got teary and replied, 'But I don't deserve it!' 'Yes, you do', said Cher. 'You're making an effort.'

The inevitable tests and trials of being a student of The Spiritual Path can lead to exhaustion, confusion, and even madness. Some students, I'm told, die on The Path. I became depressed on it.

I'd been celibate for almost two years and was happy, feeling I didn't need anyone, when Cher was given a very strong prompt to say that I was to start searching for someone in earnest. Not to start dating, but to ease the energetic wall around me that said, 'I'm unavailable.'

Around this time I began spending more time with James, an acquaintance of mine who was kind, intelligent and fun. Yet his character and lifestyle also differed from mine. Because James neglected himself physically, I'd at times be embarrassed to be around him. There was of course a reason why he was the way he was, yet I struggled to tap into my compassion – which is what my very best self required of me.

I knew I was meant to be diligent, DETERMINED and have faith in Divine Will – and I could even see the glorious opportunity being offered. But, sadly, I remained unhappy and ungrateful, and therefore unspiritual.

As a result, five years after we met, Cher said she could no longer advise me on my inner life. And thus, as yet, I have not completed my seven years of spiritual training.

SPIRITUAL UNFOLDMENT
Before this, the further I advanced in my training, the bigger the blessings that had been bestowed on me. Glimpses, I believe, of the ultimate reward of surrendering sluggish personal will to fiery Divine Will. The better, and more blessed, we are, the more we may bless others.

Healing vessel
In my first year of training, Cher revealed that people might begin to start feeling healed when they talked to me. I thought that sounded wonderful! Not for me – simply wonderful that such things happened at all.

Some time had passed when I bumped into Lorna on a night out and sat down to talk, as I knew she'd found things tough since losing her mother in very difficult circumstances. The next day I received a text saying, 'I felt quite healed just sitting and chatting with you for a few mins.'

Multidimensional love

Intrigued by Cher's instruction to 'Look out for experiences in nature,' I went to Peckham Rye Park in southeast London, near where I then lived, to rest on a wooden bench between two hedgerows.

I was sitting, enjoying the sunny scene, when I psychically saw my right ear canal extend, cartoon-like, into the privet hedge right next to me. Keeping my mind still, I observed the expansion continue until my sense of "self" included the entire garden, all four corners and everything within. Though separate to the physical eye, I experienced us as intrinsically One.

A fast-pulsed energy pattern then traversed my heart and I could feel the love – the gentle, elevated, saturated-in-kindness kind of love that I'd felt with lovers. Now my head energetically leaned out against the plant as a tear trickled out of my left eye. I was having a love-in with a hedge! Magically, I was being shown that divine love can be experienced in many forms, not just between humans.

The Divine enters

A sharp, painful release from my heart followed by an instantaneous image of a white cross over it marked the beginning of an inner journey. I then saw myself robed in white, kneeling, and offering my hands up to the Divine.

A vision of a huge angel with the most amazing feathered wings soon appeared. 'Do you fear your own light?' it asked. I felt so small and child-like in its presence that I stayed silent.

Soon I prayed for the light of the Divine to shine through me in every moment. In response came perhaps the most thrilling words I'd heard until that point: 'The Divine walks in you. Rejoice!' I didn't fully know what that meant, but needless to say, for the rest of the day I was carried on a wonderful wave of elation!

CHAPTER 12
THE DIVINE

Me: If I let go, where do I go?
The Divine: To ME, to ME, to ME!

Love changes everything. Not just for the better, but for the very best. Think of how the rose, one of the most beautiful flowers in the world, begins as a small, brown, simple seed. True love unlocks our deepest potential regardless of surface appearance.

One February I found myself walking past an elderly blind man tapping his white stick along the pavement. All around shone the bright, warm sunlight of a perfect spring-like day. His vulnerability moved me.

No matter how hard we may find life's trials, and no matter how little we see it or believe in it, the effulgent light of the Divine envelops us in every moment. The road to self-betterment, as I have come to view it, is to have our eyes opened to the mystery of divine love that is forever beckoning us to rise up and shine.

It is best to give thanks. For our life, our breath, our food, our friends, and for every single day, knowing that each one presents a new opportunity to pursue our ambitions to become the best we can be. To make a difference.

The extent to which we polish up and actively align our free will with Divine Will, which encompasses the supreme betterment of all beings, is the extent to which we experience real transformation. For we get to know the Divine *experientially*.

'One must love the Divine and not just seek or read about it. That power is what takes you to the next level of experience,' explains Cher. How do you love the Divine? Being joyful, peaceful, selfless and fearless as much as possible is a very good start.

When we go the extra mile, we are rewarded. I'd like to share an example. In one inner journey, a mermaid-like being came and led me by the hand into another dimension where a bright fire appeared. On throwing my fears into it one by one, I was instructed to sit in it. I did, and heard, 'Ask to be in the Divine Presence.' Waves of light and peace, so deep they permeated my very being, began flowing through me. Powerful waves that melted me deeper into eternal rest.

At other times, I've been commanded to stop resting. On one particular visit to my parents I had arrived after the seven-hour journey from London tired and my mind busy. In the privacy of my bedroom I soon slipped into a peaceful half-asleep, half-awake state in which I heard, 'On your knees, counsellor!' As soon as I was kneeling on my bed, the next instruction sounded, 'Stay here for two hours'. Then, 'Give your cares to Me. A life of tireless work is your destiny.'

In working to love the Divine, I have transformed, though I look the same on the outside. Life isn't all about me any more. I am being freed to focus on helping and uplifting others, including doing things for my Creator.

Today, I'm kinder, gentler, stronger, wiser. I'm also more

loving, confident, patient, generous, tolerant, self-controlled, and compassionate. I'm also aware that there is a great deal more potential within me. Just as there is in you.

But the greatest difference to before my spiritual unfoldment began is that today I focus on the higher purpose in a situation. Every day I actively look for opportunities to help others; a focus that I find endlessly uplifting. It is a beautiful way to live!

Tuning into Divine Will in this way I am freed again and again from the vicissitudes of my own will to enjoy the luxury of being directed by the all-loving Divine. With the Divine as our guide, we'll never feel down or lost again.

Unless, that is, we let go of the Divine's holy hand. All seekers let go at one point, a phase known in esoteric thinking as a dark night of the soul. And just as it was our decisions that caused us to enter it, so is it up to us to lift ourselves out of it.

Hugh, a family friend awarded an OBE for his good works as an ophthalmologist, is a tirelessly kind man. In his 80s, he still saw patients and helped others at every opportunity. Five years ago, after 49 years of loving marriage, his wife passed suddenly from a brain haemorrhage. In his grief he began to question his beliefs, thinking to himself, 'We're just like insects; we're all going to die! There's no point to life.'

Then, one heavy-hearted day that same year, he found himself opening a drawer in his desk. Inside were reams of letters from patients thanking him for changing their lives. Fortified, he changed his self-talk and declared, 'All your life you've been of service. Don't change direction now. Continue!'

Within 12 months, his faith and focus were quietly rewarded: a long-term friendship with a family friend deepened and he's now happily remarried.

To devote our life to the Divine is a choice; one we can boldly make at any time. When we forget ourselves and our wants completely, we may be rewarded with realising the magnificence of who we really are – our very best self!

This is why a spiritual life requires so much faith. What you may be asked to lose is what you hold most dear, only to discover that what you let go of was never really you anyway. Liberated from the suffocating limits of your lower self, you expand, laughing, into a higher life.

Ordinary women and men throughout history have become holy here on Earth because they endured their tests and trials with faith – *'for the water never feared the fire.'** Saints, Masters and mystics have achieved the seemingly impossible and helped countless beings live in harmony by putting Divine Will above their own. In doing so, they serve as blissful beacons lighting the eternal path to self-betterment.
*Rumi.

'The Divine will decide what to give, when to give, and where. Hence, all actions should be dedicated to the Divine,' explains Cher. 'The Divine will decide what the devotee is fit to receive. When everything is left to the Divine out of pure love and total faith, the Divine will take care of the devotee.'

Parting Note

Make peace part of your daily path
And great Love will light your inner hearth

If some of what you've read here seems fantastical, I empathise. I'd likely think the same if it hadn't happened to me. But it has.

The overriding sense with which I'm left is that the inner call to 'Come Home!' and be not just better beings, but our very *best* beings, is ultimately within us all. It is our birthright to live free of all limitations.

And so it is my heartfelt hope that, on reading this book and following the guidance offered, you go on to be, feel and do more good than you ever thought possible.

Let's pay it forward!

Recommended
Reading and Resources

General
The Sacred History: How Angels, Mystics and Higher Intelligence Made Our World by Jonathan Black (Quercus)

Harmless Diet
animalsactually.com – educational games, books and songs for children that teach them to be happy, healthy and kind to all beings
Food for a Future: The Complete Case for Vegetarianism by Jon Wynne-Tyson (Thorsons)
vegansociety.com – they run the 30-Day Vegan Challenge
veggiepets.com – Europe's largest online vegetarian petfood store
deliciouslyella.com, *minimalistbaker.com*, *greenkitchenstories.com*, *mynewroots.org* – packed with delicious meat-, dairy-, and sugar-free recipes
nationearth.com/films – creators of *Earthlings*, an award-winning documentary film about humankind's total dependence on animals for making money.

Spiritual Living and the Spiritual Path
The Hidden Secrets of a Modern Seer by Cher Chevalier (O Books)
The Hidden Truths of a Modern Seer by Cher Chevalier (Asherah Books)
Note: the third book in Cher's trilogy has not yet been published
A Little Light on the Spiritual Laws by Diana Cooper (Hodder)
Autobiography of a Yogi by Paramahansa Yogananda (Rider and Co.)
Brother of the Third Degree by Will L Garver (Cornerstone Book Publishers)

The Initiate: Some Impressions of a Great Soul by Cyril Scott (Red Wheel/Weiser)

The Initiate in the Dark Cycle by Cyril Scott (Red Wheel/Weiser)

The Initiate in the New World by Cyril Scott (Red Wheel/Weiser)

Daughter of Fire: A Diary of a Spiritual Training with a Sufi Master by Irina Tweedie (Golden Sufi Centre)

In The Outer Court by Annie Besant (The Theosophical Publishing Society)

The Spiritual Life by Annie Besant (Quest)

The Gnostic Gospels by Alan Jacobs (Watkins)

Practical Mysticism by Evelyn Underhill (Wilder Publications)

The Holy Bible: Douay-Rheims Version (Baronius Press)

LIFE-TRANSFORMATION WORKSHOPS

thejourney.com

pathoflove.net

Both organisations hold regular workshops and trainings all over the world

OVERCOMING NEGATIVITY

You Can't Afford the Luxury of a Negative Thought: A Guide to Positive Thinking by John-Roger and Peter McWilliams (Thorsons)

PRAYER

Mystics at Prayer by Many Cihlar and H Spencer Lewis (Kessinger Publishing)

The Practice of the Presence of God and the Spiritual Maxims by Brother Lawrence (Dover Publications)

RELATIONSHIPS

Soul Mates and Twin Flames: The Spiritual Dimension of Love and Relationships by Elizabeth Clare Prophet (Summit University Press)
See also *A Little Light on The Spiritual Laws*

SOMATIC EXPERIENCE TRAUMA THERAPY

Waking the Tiger: Healing trauma by Peter A Levine (North Atlantic Books)
In an Unspoken Voice: How the body releases trauma and restores goodness by Peter A Levine (North Atlantic Books)
The Body Keeps the Score: Mind, brain and body in the transformation of trauma by Bessel van der Kolk (Penguin)
To find a Somatic Experiencing practitioner (SEP), search the registry at *traumahealing.com* (worldwide) or *seauk.org.uk* (UK only). Both list the professional SE trainings.

15102871R00060

Printed in Poland
by Amazon Fulfillment
Poland Sp. z o.o., Wrocław